S. Hrg. 115–132

CONSUMER DATA SECURITY AND THE CREDIT BUREAUS

HEARING

BEFORE THE

COMMITTEE ON
BANKING, HOUSING, AND URBAN AFFAIRS
UNITED STATES SENATE

ONE HUNDRED FIFTEENTH CONGRESS

FIRST SESSION

ON

EXAMINING THE PROTECTION OF CONSUMER DATA AT CREDIT
BUREAUS IN THE WAKE OF THE EQUIFAX DATA BREACH

OCTOBER 17, 2017

Printed for the use of the Committee on Banking, Housing, and Urban Affairs

Available at: http://www.govinfo.gov/

U.S. GOVERNMENT PUBLISHING OFFICE

28–249 PDF　　　　WASHINGTON : 2018

For sale by the Superintendent of Documents, U.S. Government Publishing Office
Internet: bookstore.gpo.gov　Phone: toll free (866) 512–1800; DC area (202) 512–1800
Fax: (202) 512–2104　Mail: Stop IDCC, Washington, DC 20402–0001

C O N T E N T S

TUESDAY, OCTOBER 17, 2017

CONSUMER DATA SECURITY AND THE CREDIT BUREAUS

TUESDAY, OCTOBER 17, 2017

U.S. SENATE,
COMMITTEE ON BANKING, HOUSING, AND URBAN AFFAIRS,
Washington, DC.

The Committee met at 10:03 a.m., in room SD–538, Dirksen Senate Office Building, Hon. Mike Crapo, Chairman of the Committee, presiding.

OPENING STATEMENT OF CHAIRMAN MIKE CRAPO

Chairman CRAPO. This Committee will come to order.

As a follow-up to our hearing on the Equifax data breach, today we will receive testimony on the protection of consumer data at credit bureaus.

At the Equifax hearing, Members expressed interest in better understanding how credit bureaus are regulated, how they protect consumer data, and whether there are gaps that Congress needs to fill.

I have long been concerned about the ever increasing amounts of "big data" collected by companies and by the Government. It is critical that personal data is protected, consumer impact in the event of a breach is minimized, and consumers' ability to access credit is not harmed.

Credit bureaus play a valuable role in our financial system by helping financial institutions assess a consumer's ability to meet financial obligations and also facilitating access to beneficial financial products and services.

The inherent nature of the credit bureau business, as with most businesses in this digital age, requires utmost data security measures to ensure that sensitive consumer information is safeguarded.

Two weeks ago, Equifax testified about the methods it uses to protect its consumer data bases, such as encryption at rest and tokenization. Former Equifax CEO Richard Smith noted that while some of Equifax's data bases are encrypted at rest, the dispute portal that was compromised was not.

Questions remain about the best ways to protect sensitive data, including:

Are there data security industry standards and best practices at credit bureaus?

Should tools like encryption at rest be employed to protect all data containing sensitive consumer information?

What role do financial institutions and Federal agencies play in data security at credit bureaus?

Given that credit bureaus are financial institutions under the Gramm–Leach–Bliley Act, how does data security, testing, and oversight by regulators compare to that of traditional financial institutions?

I look forward to hearing from our witnesses about what credit bureaus do to ensure security for the data they collect, who oversees credit bureaus to ensure they have adequate security measures in place, and what improvements could be made to the oversight of data security at the credit bureaus.

There are also many concerns regarding company response to data breaches. The Equifax breach has left more than 145 million consumers a little confused as to what can be done to mitigate damage to their identities and credit.

We do know that starting in January, Equifax will offer all customers the ability to lock or unlock their credit files for free.

Additional products have also been offered from Equifax and the other credit bureaus for consumers to monitor or freeze their credit reports.

Many consumers remain confused about which options are best for them, but this hearing will hopefully provide some additional clarity. We have a shared interest on this Committee in ensuring that credit bureaus take the necessary measures to safeguard personal data and minimize risk of another massive data breach.

Senator Brown.

OPENING STATEMENT OF SENATOR SHERROD BROWN

Senator BROWN. Thank you, Chairman Crapo.

Under current law, whether we like it or not, companies like Equifax can collect vast troves of personal information. That includes information plucked from our work histories, our social media profiles, from reward cards that track our purchases at the grocery store, and even information from our cell phones tracking our daily commutes.

Generally, these companies are free to combine and sell that information to all sorts of financial institutions and other data mining firms who use it to make decisions about us—like what kind of car or job that we might get.

Corporations like Equifax rarely have to tell us exactly why or how these decisions are made. They get to hide behind proprietary models and trade secrets. It seems our laws protect big corporations' use of people's data a lot better than they actually protect people.

As the recent breach demonstrates, enhanced cybersecurity measures at companies like Equifax might work perfectly yet still do little to protect consumers' data. While 145 million people have had their private data exposed, it does not appear that any sensitive corporate data was accessed.

Because these businesses are not accountable to consumers, and because consumers have no choice over who is collecting their information, consumer protection is pretty much an afterthought.

As we talk about the clearly inadequate protections for consumer data at Equifax and those in place at the other consumer reporting agencies today, we cannot forget that the real victims of this hack are the 145 million people—5 million in my State alone—who, through no fault of their own, have had their personal information compromised.

I hope that at today's hearing we do not just talk about how we strengthen cybersecurity. We do need to do that, of course, but we also need to explore how to restore people's control over their own information. We need to examine whether the current credit bureau model makes sense for American consumers.

We know the credit bureaus have a long history of consumer complaints and inaccurate reporting that has long-term effects on people's ability to get a job or get a house. Rather than addressing these problems, the credit bureaus have spent millions acquiring other data collection companies and branching out into new lines of business.

Despite their continued failure—there is no other word to use— their continued failure to provide accurate credit reporting services or to protect all of the data that they collect, their CEOs have been rewarded with enormous salaries and bonuses. Sometimes they come in front of us and say they are going to give up their bonus, as if that is a major concession. Now, in an era of nonstop cyberthreats, it seems like they have made consumers even more vulnerable.

Equifax made astounding amounts of money off of the consumer data it collected; and unless things change, it looks like it will hardly pay a price for its recklessness. It is still collecting and storing our data, and in some cases we are even giving it tax dollars to do it. I look forward to today's witnesses' views on these matters.

Thank you.

Chairman CRAPO. Thank you, Senator Brown. We will now turn to our witnesses.

First, we will receive testimony from Mr. Andrew Smith, partner at Covington & Burling, on behalf of the Consumer Data Industry Association.

Then we will hear from Mr. Marc Rotenberg, president of the Electronic Privacy Information Center.

And, finally, we will hear from Mr. Chris Jaikaran. Did I pronounce that right?

Mr. JAIKARAN. Jaikaran.

Chairman CRAPO. Jaikaran. Thank you. Mr. Chris Jaikaran, Analyst in Cybersecurity Policy at the Congressional Research Service.

Each witness is recognized for 5 minutes of oral remarks, and then we will proceed to questions. Mr. Smith, you may proceed.

STATEMENT OF ANDREW M. SMITH, PARTNER, COVINGTON & BURLING LLP, ON BEHALF OF THE CONSUMER DATA INDUSTRY ASSOCIATION

Mr. SMITH. Thank you. Chairman Crapo, Ranking Member Brown, and Members of the Committee, thank you for the opportunity to appear before you. My name is Andrew Smith, and I am a partner at the law firm Covington & Burling. I am appearing today on behalf of the Consumer Data Industry Association, which is a trade association of companies that provide businesses with the information and analytical tools necessary to manage risk and to protect consumers. CDIA's members include the three national credit bureaus: Equifax, Experian, and TransUnion.

You have asked us to discuss how credit bureaus protect consumer data, but first I wanted to mention the important role played by the national credit reporting system in our economy. More than two-thirds of our GDP comes from consumer spending, fueled by consumer credit. It is the national credit reporting system that allows consumers to quickly and effortlessly open a bank account or purchase a cell phone. More than 40 percent of consumers move every year, and the national credit reporting system facilitates this mobility, in addition to providing fast, fair, and impartial access to well-priced credit, insurance, apartment rental, and other essential services.

Nearly 50 years ago, Congress enacted the Fair Credit Reporting Act to ensure the fairness and impartiality of credit reports, to protect consumer privacy, and to foster the continued development and vitality of the national credit reporting system.

The most recent revision to this comprehensive regulatory scheme was the addition of the CFPB as a supervisory agency. This is the first agency to directly supervise the national credit reporting system, not just examining credit bureaus but also examining the users of credit reports and the companies that contribute information into the credit bureaus. The CFPB's virtual continuous supervision of the credit reporting system began in earnest in early 2012 and, according to the CFPB, has produced, and I quote, "a proactive approach to compliance management" that "will reap benefits for consumers—and for lenders—for many years to come."

With respect to data security, credit bureaus are subject to Federal and State laws requiring them to safeguard consumer data, and because of the key role they play in the banking system, they also are subject to very specific private data security requirements, such as the payment card industry data security standards.

To begin, credit bureaus are required by the FCRA to maintain procedures to ensure that they only provide credit reports to legitimate people for legitimate purposes. These credentialing requirements go beyond contractual certifications and include comprehensive due diligence of prospective customers as well as continuous monitoring of existing customers.

The FCRA also requires secure disposal of credit report information. In addition, the FTC's Safeguards Rule, as referred to by Chairman Crapo, under the Gramm–Leach–Bliley Act requires financial institutions, including credit bureaus, to develop and implement comprehensive information security programs. The laws of at least 13 States similarly require companies to implement and maintain reasonable procedures to safeguard sensitive personal information. Furthermore, almost every State requires that companies notify consumers when there is unauthorized access to or acquisition of sensitive personal information.

Because of their important role in the banking system, credit bureaus are also subject to private contractual data security requirements. For example, because the credit bureaus handle credit card information, the card networks—Visa, MasterCard, et cetera—require that they comply with the payment card industry data security standards and validate such compliance by obtaining an independent third-party audit of their security procedures. In addition, because banks provide a great deal of sensitive customer information to the national credit bureaus, they are required by their prudential regulators to conduct regular information security audits of the credit bureaus. These audits can include onsite inspections which might last for several days. Each of the three national credit bureaus is subject to dozens of these bank reviews each year.

CDIA shares with you the goal of ensuring that consumers and businesses have confidence in the ability of the national credit reporting system to keep consumer data safe.

Thank you for the opportunity to testify, and we look forward to today's dialogue.

Chairman CRAPO. Thank you.

Mr. Rotenberg.

STATEMENT OF MARC ROTENBERG, PRESIDENT, ELECTRONIC PRIVACY INFORMATION CENTER

Mr. ROTENBERG. Chairman Crapo, Ranking Member Brown, Members of the Senate Banking Committee, thank you for the opportunity to speak with you today. My name is Marc Rotenberg. I am president of the Electronic Privacy Information Center. We are an independent nonprofit research organization founded in 1994 to focus public attention on emerging privacy issues.

I would like to begin by saying that the Equifax data breach is one of the most serious in our Nation's history, on par with the 2015 data breach at the Office of Personnel Management that impacted more than 22.5 million Federal employees, their families, and friends. The Equifax breach poses enormous challenges to the security of American families and even to our Nation's security.

There is no simple solution, but in my testimony today I will outline the steps that I believe Congress can take to mitigate the risks that follow from the breach and reduce the danger and likelihood of future data breaches.

I should also say that the Equifax breach is remarkable because of its scope, the sensitivity of the data, and the delay to fix a well-documented security flaw. More than 4 months passed from the time Equifax failed to install critical software updates, and the data that was disclosed is precisely the information that individuals rely upon to open bank accounts, get car loans, seek employment, and buy cell phones. The data included names, Social Security numbers, birth dates, home addresses, and driver's license information. This is also the data that criminals use to commit identity theft and financial fraud.

Equifax is clearly responsible for this breach. The company was notified in March by both the Apache Software Foundation and U.S.–CERT of the need to make critical software changes. But it is also worth emphasizing that Equifax chose to collect this personal data on American consumers. Consumers did not provide this information to Equifax. And the lax security strategy that they followed meant that a single breach resulted in the release of 145 million credit reports on American consumers.

The breach will cause unprecedented harm. When hackers get access to credit card numbers, consumers can cancel accounts and change the credit card numbers. But it is not so easy to change a

Social Security number, and I do not think it is possible to change your date of birth. Equifax's victims will be exposed to the ongoing risk of identity theft and financial fraud, which is already an enormous problem for American consumers. The FTC reported almost 400,000 cases of identity theft in the United States in 2016; 29 percent of those cases involved tax fraud, and the Department of Justice estimates the cost to the U.S. economy at over $15 billion per year.

The credit reporting industry is in urgent need of reform. In my testimony I have outlined a number of steps that I believe should be taken to establish accountability and transparency. Most simply, consumers need to be given greater control about the information about them that impacts their financial future.

This means, for example, that we should have a nationwide credit freeze, or to say a little bit more precisely, the disclosure of credit reports should be on an opt-in basis. We recognize the value of credit in the American economy, but it is the consumer who should decide when it is in their interest to disclose their information to a third party to obtain a car loan. They should not have to jump through hoops to put in blocks and freezes to restrict access by others. They should make the affirmative decision.

Credit monitoring should also be freely available. You should not have to pay to be told that there is a fraudulent activity on your account, but that is the current problem with credit monitoring services that require either a fee or limit the access to credit monitoring for 90 days. This makes no sense whatsoever. If there is a problem in the account, the consumer should be notified.

We also think consumers should have more ready access to the contents of the credit report so they know who is receiving the information and the impact that the data might have.

I have several other suggestions in my testimony, which I would be pleased to provide for the Committee.

Thank you.

Chairman CRAPO. Thank you.

Mr. Jaikaran.

STATEMENT OF CHRIS JAIKARAN, ANALYST IN CYBERSECURITY POLICY, CONGRESSIONAL RESEARCH SERVICE

Mr. JAIKARAN. Chairman Crapo, Ranking Member Brown, and Members of the Committee, thank you for the opportunity to testify on consumer data security and the credit bureaus. My name is Chris Jaikaran, and I am an Analyst in Cybersecurity Policy at the Congressional Research Service. In this role, I research and analyze cybersecurity issues and their policy implications, including issues of data security, protection, and management.

My written statement for the record goes into further detail, but my testimony today will address data security as an element of cybersecurity and risk management, cyberincident response, and options for Congress to address data security.

An increasingly used catchphrase among industry analysts is that today "all companies are technology companies" or "all companies are data companies." This concept reflects that information technology and data play an important role in enabling the modern business practices which allow companies to compete and thrive in the marketplace. However, this reliance on IT and data also creates risk for corporate leadership to manage. Adequately controlling that risk is an objective of cybersecurity.

Data security is an element of cybersecurity that involves risk management. Absolute security is not obtainable, so managing the risks which would impair security is the goal. In order to evaluate risk, managers need to understand the threats their enterprise may face, the vulnerabilities they have, and the consequences of an incident.

Cybersecurity incident response describes activities to confirm an attack, discover information about it, and mitigate against it.

For incident response, staff is not limited to just IT personnel. Communications staff that are able to craft messages to both internal and external stakeholders, legal teams who can help with reporting and compliance requirements, and management and corporate boards who are accountable for the operations of a corporation should all be included in response planning, among others, depending on the entity.

There will be a delay between the discovery of an attack and the public notification of that attack because analysis of what transpired will need to be conducted. This analysis will inform the entity of how they were breached and what data or systems were compromised. This type of analysis may be conducted by the entity itself, a business partner of the entity, Government response teams, and law enforcement. With a variety of potential forensic investigators, determining how they will coordinate in their response and how they will share information among one another is a factor which should be determined during the planning and training phase. With information on how the breach happened and the extent of the breach, the entity can proceed to mitigate its effects. These phases need not occur in succession, but may be able to occur concurrently.

I will now briefly present three options Congress could consider to address data security.

Congress could explicitly authorize a Federal regulator to examine credit reporting agencies for their adherence to the Safeguards Rule, as promulgated by the Federal Trade Commission. The dialogue created by the Federal Government and credit reporting agencies could lead to greater understand of the cybersecurity risk faced by credit reporting agencies and allow for those with deficiencies to correct their security posture prior to referral for enforcement action.

Congress could regulate the collection, use, and retention of data regardless of the type of entity that houses that data. The European Union and Canada have such data laws.

Congress can establish requirements on what data may be collected, how data must be stored, and the consumer's rights to collection and use of data about them.

Congress could require credit reporting agencies, or any entity that profits from consumer data, to identify and disclose their data model to consumers. Elements such as where data is acquired, how it is used, and what other data the entity generates about the consumer will provide consumers with additional information that may affect their decisions in the marketplace.

Thank you for the opportunity to testify today, and I look forward to your questions.

Chairman CRAPO. Thank you very much.

Before I begin my questions, just to inform the Senators, we have a vote at 10:30. Senator Brown and I have discussed it, and we intend to keep the hearing running, so we will adjust our attendance at the vote, and you can make your plans accordingly. But the hearing will continue to proceed during the vote.

The first question I have is for the whole panel, and I am going to ask you to be concise. I only have 5 minutes in my questioning, as does each of the other Senators. But this is for each of the Members of the panel, if you have an opinion on this.

There has been a lot of discussion surrounding the security of the Social Security number and whether it should be used as an identifier going forward. Do you think we need to get rid of the Social Security number as a personal identifier? And if so, what viable alternatives do we have? How would we ensure that such an alternative does not suffer from the same drawbacks as the Social Security number? Mr. Smith, do you want to start?

Mr. SMITH. I think that if we eliminate the Social Security number as a personal identifier, we are going to have to have something, some other unique identifier that will allow businesses, credit bureaus, others to know who precisely they are dealing with. So my name is Andrew Smith. There are thousands of me, perhaps tens of thousands of me. When you are looking at a bankruptcy court record, if there is no identifier on there, how do you know which Andrew Smith it is?

So Socials right now, and other identifiers, play a critical role in the economy, just simple identification, right? Not authentication, not verification, not that I truly am who I say I am. From that perspective, Socials are terrible. But as identifiers, Socials have had a role to play.

Whether we need another identifier, I think that we are willing to work with you on that to try to get to the right result for consumers.

Chairman CRAPO. Mr. Rotenberg.

Mr. ROTENBERG. Thank you for the question. I have spent many years before many congressional committees urging that limits be established on the use of the Social Security number, but we have never argued for replacing the Social Security number. The key point is that the SSN serves an important purpose in the management of certain Government record systems. That is what it was established for, and that is where the legal authority exists.

The problem is that the SSN was adopted in the private sector and used as an identifier for general purposes. This has actually contributed to identity theft and financial fraud. It is an imperfect identifier. It is used both as a password and as an authenticator. It was intended really for neither. So when we talk about the Social Security number, we would not say replace the SSN. As I describe in my testimony, we would say limit the use of the SSN. It should only be available in the private sector for lawful purposes.

Chairman CRAPO. Thank you.

Mr. Jaikaran.

Mr. JAIKARAN. The Social Security number is a piece of personally identifiable information, so limiting its use in the private sector may lead to reduce consequences that impact if there is a data breach. However, whatever replaces it would likely still remain personally identifiable information that would constitute some level of increased security posture around that data in case there were a breach.

Chairman CRAPO. Thank you. And this question is also just for you, Mr. Jaikaran. Your testimony discusses encryption and other tools that can be used in providing data security. Equifax's former CEO mentioned that some of their data is encrypted at rest while some of it is not. Are there certain minimum data security tools or standards that should be employed across the board for data sets containing personally identifiable information? Are there measures that, if in place, may have been able to prevent the Equifax breach or detected it sooner?

Mr. JAIKARAN. So in my testimony I discuss cybersecurity as an element of risk management, understanding the entire risk that an enterprise or a corporation may face in their conduct of their business. There is Federal guidance that is created for the implementation of encryption, and there are industry best practices on the use of encryption for data at rest, data in motion, or data in process. While these may exist, a lot depends on how it is implemented and the use cases of each individual company for where they apply that encryption, how strictly they apply it, and how the keys are managed within that enterprise to allow those with legitimate access to continue to be able to conduct the business while still restricting access to those that do not.

Chairman CRAPO. All right. Thank you very much. And I just have about 45 seconds left, so, Mr. Smith and Mr. Rotenberg, very briefly, under the current legal framework, the FTC has enforcement authority over its Safeguards Rule for data security, but no regulatory agency currently examines or supervises credit bureaus for data security, as is the case with banks.

Do you think there is a gap in this framework? And do we need an agency to be set up or authorized to examine for data security?

Mr. SMITH. So as you noted, the FTC has law enforcement authority, and we feel as though we are not unsupervised with respect to data security. We do, as I said earlier, have our bank customers who are regularly auditing us. I would say, however, that if there are gaps in supervision, we would be happy to talk with you about that and to come up with the most sensible result for consumers.

Chairman CRAPO. All right. Thank you.

Mr. Rotenberg, very quickly.

Mr. ROTENBERG. The FTC Safeguards Rule is an important data security standard, but it only applies right now after the fact. The FTC can only act against a credit reporting agency once the breach occurs. We think they should have the ability before the breach to inspect and determine compliance with standards.

Chairman CRAPO. Thank you.

Senator Brown.

Senator BROWN. Thank you, Mr. Chairman.

Mr. Smith, in your testimony you stated the credit reporting system "provides critically important benefits," and you went on to say it is "indispensable to the economy." I think we all agree with that, so my questions are this, and I will start with you, Mr. Jaikaran, and please give a "yes" or "no" on this, if possible. Do you think that the breach or failure of a nationwide credit reporting agency, whether it is Equifax or TransUnion or Experian, do you think that a breach or failure of one of those agencies could have a systematic—or, I am sorry, could have a systemic impact on the U.S. financial system?

Mr. JAIKARAN. A breach of any agency is difficult to judge, depending on the categorization of the agency itself, but it is a possibility that it could have impacts on the financial system.

Senator BROWN. Mr. Rotenberg.

Mr. ROTENBERG. I think the answer is clearly yes.

Senator BROWN. Mr. Smith.

Mr. SMITH. I think that with respect to the Equifax incident, one of the things that we need to keep in mind is that, according to the news reports, the credit reporting data base was not, in fact, compromised. A compromise of a credit reporting data base, I would have to think about whether it would present——

Senator BROWN. So you are the one that started off by saying it provides critically important benefits, it is indispensable to the economy, then a breach of 145 million you do not think does have a systemic impact on the U.S. financial system?

Mr. SMITH. I think that the risk would be able to be managed by banks, but I do think that it is going to be something that would need to be actively managed, because what it would present——

Senator BROWN. Is that a "yes" or a "no" to systemic impact? "Could be managed." A lot of things could be managed. Does that have a systemic impact on the financial system, as the two gentlemen to your——

Mr. SMITH. I am not prepared——

Senator BROWN. ——left said yes.

Mr. SMITH. I am not prepared to say that it would have a systemic impact, but I would like to think that through.

Senator BROWN. OK. Could you in the next week let me know if that is a "yes" or "no"?

Mr. SMITH. Sure. How would you define "systemic impact"?

Senator BROWN. Well, I am asking you to.

Mr. SMITH. OK.

Senator BROWN. 145 million sounds systemic to me. A No. One-fifth that does.

Mr. Rotenberg, most of us or our family members have faced challenges for decades trying to fix inaccuracies in their credit reports. These inaccuracies result in Equifax or TransUnion or Experian being three of the most complained about companies to the CFPB. Do you think it would make sense to prevent these consumer reporting agencies from collecting new personal data or providing other services until they have met an accuracy metric in their consumer credit reporting? And second question, related, should consumers be allowed access to all the data held by these three companies?

Mr. ROTENBERG. Senator, I think both suggestions are very good. I think credit reporting agencies which provide personal data to others should be held to an accuracy standard because, of course, when they provide information that is inaccurate, incomplete, or out of date, people are wrongfully denied credit, they are wrongfully denied jobs, and that is certainly a problem.

But also, to your second point, whatever information the credit reporting agencies know about us, I think we should have the right to know, particularly now when this information is being made available for sale for data brokers and oftentimes falls outside the protections of the Fair Credit Reporting Act. I think we need to do much more to give consumers information and control about their personal information held by others.

Senator BROWN. Thank you.

Mr. Smith, consumer advocates have called for free security freezes to be provided by Equifax and TransUnion and Experian. Instead, the companies have announced that they are rolling out what are called "credit lock products," which appear to give consumers fewer rights and less security than credit freezes.

Are CRAs offering credit locks so consumers have to sign forced arbitration agreements just like they had to on Equifax's first offer of credit monitoring products?

Mr. SMITH. So can I respond really quickly to the issue of access? I wanted to remind the Members of the Committee that consumers do have access to all of the information on file about them with consumer reporting agencies, and they have free access to that through annualcreditreport.com as well as through other mechanisms.

With respect to——

Senator BROWN. Access and correcting are two different phenomena, but go ahead.

Mr. SMITH. Yeah, yeah, and they have——

Senator BROWN. But answer the question I asked.

Mr. SMITH. ——dispute and correct. And with respect to the credit locks, I am not so familiar with the different features of the credit locks, nor do I know whether they have an arbitration clause——

Senator BROWN. You do know they did, though, on the first round of credit monitoring products that they, let us say, quote-unquote, generously offered——

Mr. SMITH. Right, I know——

Senator BROWN. ——they included that, as you know.

Mr. SMITH. Yes.

Senator BROWN. They backed off it under public pressure, as you also know.

Mr. SMITH. That I know. I do not think that the impetus for offering credit locks would be to obtain a mandatory arbitration clause from consumers. I do think that these credit locks may be useful to consumers. I think that freezes more generally serve a specific need for a specific type of consumer. There are a lot of other tools that consumers have that can protect themselves in these situations, including obtaining a free credit report, placing a fraud alert on their credit report, obtaining credit monitoring. There is a lot of free credit monitoring available. So I think consumers should understand and appreciate that before they place a credit freeze on their file. But credit freezes do have their place.

Senator BROWN. I do not want to debate that, but I will just close with on the forced arbitration agreement, you are their lawyer. You represent them. They also rely on you for advice. Are you willing to go back to them and say that there is strong sentiment among the public and this Congress that forced arbitration agreements should not be part of this credit lock offered products?

Mr. SMITH. Yes, I will convey that message. I do think that there is a special—there is sort of an exigent circumstance when we are talking about credit monitoring and other credit report-related products, and there is a statute called the "Credit Repair Organizations Act" which imposes particularly stringent penalties on companies, any company that is found to be a credit repair organization. And so because of that—and I think some Members of the Committee are probably familiar with this. Because of that, arbitration clauses have a special role to play with these products. But I will certainly convey the message that——

Senator BROWN. Would you share with the Committee exactly what message you convey to them on forced arbitration?

Mr. SMITH. I will share that.

Senator BROWN [presiding]. Thank you.

Senator Rounds.

Senator ROUNDS. Thank you.

Gentlemen, regardless of what we put into law, regardless of what rules are put in place, if they are not followed, the possibilities of an additional breach continue. I am just curious. With regard to Equifax, would it be fair to say that the data that we have so far, the information that we have so far, does it point to basically human error having been the cause of the data breach? I would like just a quick response from each.

Mr. ROTENBERG. Senator, I think human error understates the problem. We are talking about a breach that impacted 145 million records, a circumstance where the company was twice notified by two leading authorities and left the breach exposed over a 4-month period. I did not discuss it in my testimony this morning, but even the response to the breach was not helpful to consumers. So at almost every step, they did the wrong thing by consumers.

Mr. SMITH. I believe that Equifax has said publicly that it was the result of human error with respect to the question about human error. I would add, though, that the FTC and CFPB are investigating the breach, and I would want to see what their conclusions are before we draw any broader—before we make any policy choices based on the fact of this breach.

Senator ROUNDS. Mr. Jaikaran.

Mr. JAIKARAN. Based on the amount of information that we have regarding this particular breach, it is difficult to judge as to whether the breach came down to human error or some other reason within the company. So it is difficult to judge at this point based on the information we have.

Senator ROUNDS. Let us assume that there was human error involved in this, recognizing the significant damage that has been caused. If we have within our abilities the opportunity to lay out a plan in which there is not just an auditable but a review process that could be put in place with assurances of the follow-through, we are still talking about the protections that we put in place for a legal entity that has been breached by thieves.

What more can we do or what more should we be doing to prevent this break-in in the first place with regard to protections and also the consequences for entities throughout the world that actually cause these breaches, that are actually overtly out trying to get their hands on the data? Do we need to look at additional Federal authorizations or institutions that would be literally for the cybercommunity, the same as the FBI was when it came to stopping the bank robberies of the 1920s and 1930s? Do we need to be looking at something like that on a worldwide basis?

Mr. ROTENBERG. Senator, I think this is a very important point. When the Fair Credit Reporting Act was passed in 1970, the primary concern was about the possible misuse of consumer data by the credit reporting agencies, and that was the problem that Congress sought to address.

But here we are, almost 50 years later, living in a world of constant cyberattack, and in my testimony this morning I tried to explain that the Equifax breach needs to be understood not just in terms of the misuse of personal data, but actually the exploitation by foreign adversaries. And that is also the reason, sir, why I think we need to update our privacy laws, put more incentives on companies to protect this data, not just from misuse but also from exploitation by foreign Governments.

Senator ROUNDS. Mr. Smith.

Mr. SMITH. We think that, to the extent that there are gaps in supervision of data security, that we are—that we want to talk with you about that. We want to get to the right result.

With respect to Professor Rotenberg's point, there is no doubt that this was a criminal hack, that it was from an unknown source, that it may have been from a foreign actor, and that is something that I think hopefully the FTC and CFPB and the other continued investigations will reveal. And if there are policy implications from that, hopefully we can have that discussion then.

Senator ROUNDS. Mr. Jaikaran.

Mr. JAIKARAN. So when we think about the Government relationship with these agencies, there are kind of three buckets that we could put them in: first is rulemaking, which the Federal Trade Commission did with the Safeguards Rule; next is examination; and the third is enforcement, which the FTC retains.

In this space we could see that the examination space was the one that we had the least Government involvement, so I think there presents an opportunity for Congress to create further guidance on how they want agencies to act with regard to that.

Concerning the consequences side, to the best of my knowledge, attribution still has not been placed for this breach, and that would be a conversation to have with law enforcement agencies and officials on what authorities they think they need in order to go after the criminals here.

Senator ROUNDS. See, I think it is important that we recognize that there is a standard of security which has to be imposed, and we have got to be able to audit it, follow through, and with consequences, but also with a continued surveillance. But until we get down to the point where there are actually consequences for the bad guys involved, we are not going to make the major dent that we have to in terms of cybertheft elsewhere. And I think we miss that sometimes. We are focusing on the people who are trying to provide services. We are not focusing on going after the guys who are actually causing the problems for everybody else, not just in the United States but elsewhere around the world as well.

Thank you, Mr. Chairman.

Senator BROWN. Senator Reed.

Senator REED. Thank you, Mr. Chairman.

Mr. Rotenberg, my sense from your testimony is that—and you can confirm this—there are two points at which consumers should have legal rights, and one is that they should have the legal right to withhold or divulge their credit score, or they should know the credit information that an agency has, and that should be by law, not by deference of the agency. Is that your view?

Mr. ROTENBERG. Yes, that is correct, Senator. When the information is being provided in the credit report, presumably it is for the consumer's benefit. They are seeking the loan. They want to buy the car. They need the mortgage. They should know when that is happening, and they should know the information that is contained in the report.

Senator REED. And that should be by statute, not by deference?

Mr. ROTENBERG. Yes. Part of this is about changing the default. Right now your credit report is freely available to others within the stricture of the Fair Credit Reporting Act, but you have very little control over that. We would say give the consumer opt-in control.

Senator REED. And Mr. Smith indicated that consumers once a year have access to all the information that a credit bureau has. Is that——

Mr. ROTENBERG. Well, it is true. Once a year they can get a free copy of their credit report. It is not all the information they have. They do not know who has received the information. And as I said, this is also a rapidly evolving industry. There are a lot of related practices that are not covered by the FCRA, and as a consequence, consumers do not have the full picture.

Senator REED. So, essentially, they could get the number, whatever it is, 400 or 800, and——

Mr. ROTENBERG. Yes.

Senator REED. And supplemental information to that number. But if, as Senator Brown suggested, the agency was also buying cell phone information or something like that, that is not——

Mr. ROTENBERG. That would fall outside of the credit report.

Senator REED. So that in order to give a citizen the full benefits, all information the agency has on them should be disclosable. Is that correct?

Mr. ROTENBERG. Yes, Senator. That is why we recommended a comprehensive approach based on a Federal baseline. It would give consumers more information about them that is being transferred to third parties.

Senator REED. And I also presume that you would suggest that they have the right to deny access to certain information.

Mr. ROTENBERG. Absolutely.

Senator REED. Or, in fact, even to require that information be deleted from the credit bureau's files.

Mr. ROTENBERG. I think many American consumers would actually be surprised to know how many people, how many businesses get access to their credit reports without their knowledge. Those reports move very freely with very little information being provided to consumers, and I think that should change.

Senator REED. In the description of what took place, it appears that there was negligence on behalf of Equifax, you know, being told by a Federal regulator to make a patch and not making the patch for several months. Does anyone have the right to sue or to enforce criminally or administratively?

Mr. ROTENBERG. Well, I am sure there will be lawsuits brought, and there are a variety of different theories. But as others have already pointed out, almost immediately Equifax's response was to try to deny consumers the opportunity to pursue their legal remedies, and that cannot be the right response.

Senator REED. But with respect to regulatory agencies, the impression that I have from the discussion is that it is all sort of retrospective, after the fact, that they can go in and make a judgment. Could the FTC levy a fine based upon failure to solve——

Mr. ROTENBERG. Actually, no. Under the Safeguards Rule, they can inspect and they can, I think, sanction. But I think a fine would require a subsequent violation of the settlement or order with the company, and the FTC under the Safeguards Rule currently would not have the ability to inspect or prevent prior to the breach occurring.

Senator REED. So under existing law, is there any way for an appropriate Federal agency to levy a fine or some type of significant penalty on the company to deter or to——

Mr. ROTENBERG. I think for the FTC to levy a fine, they would have to find a breach under the Fair Credit Reporting Act. Under Section 5 of the FTC Act, they have to have a consent order and then a subsequent violation. It is not a very effective enforcement regime.

Senator REED. I concur. Thank you very much.

Senator BROWN. Senator Scott.

Senator SCOTT. Thank you, sir. And good morning to the panel. Thank you all for being here this morning.

The Equifax breach is still catastrophic for so many in South Carolina. If you think about the numbers of individuals impacted by the breach in my home State of South Carolina, 2.4 million South Carolinians had their personal information exposed, stolen, through the Equifax breach. We only have about 5 million folks living in the State. That is about 48.76 percent of the State. That is the sixth highest number in the country. When you account for the fact that there are about 500,000 South Carolinians under the age of 14, that means that the number surges over 50 percent. So over half of the adult population at least in the State had their information exposed.

Equifax's negligence has been devastating for my constituents. But when you look at the geographic location of that impact, the Southeast region seems to have been impacted aggressively in high levels: Georgia, around 51.6 percent; Virginia, around 48.8 percent; Florida, around 53.5 percent.

I asked Equifax why South Carolina and the Southeastern region was so hard hit. I hope they find an answer soon. My suspicion is that perhaps the location, the physical location of Equifax may have played a role in that.

Mr. Jaikaran, why are the numbers so high so close to the physical headquarters of Equifax?

Mr. JAIKARAN. So that would be difficult to judge based on publicly available information, but there might be some business reasons why Equifax would have additional information on people in the Southeast region of the Nation. They may have more business partners with businesses near their headquarters, so there is a greater opportunity for sharing of information. It may be that the population of those States are prime targets for credit, so just the population of the States, the sample pool may be more amenable to a credit rating agency.

Senator SCOTT. Thank you. Things get complicated when a company is headquartered in New Jersey, does business in South Carolina, and is breached in Arkansas. These States have very different laws on the books governing when and how companies must notify the public of a data breach.

Back to you, Mr. Jaikaran. Is our current State-by-State patchwork of regulatory approaches effective in protecting the public?

Mr. JAIKARAN. Thank you, Senator. I believe my colleagues at the Government Accountability Office, or GAO, would be in a better position to evaluate the State-by-State regulatory regime we have today. However, as a broader data breach notification policy, that does provide a level of certainty for both businesses and consumers if there was a Federal rule or a Federal law on the data breach notification that is expected both for businesses to provide as well as what consumers can expect to receive.

Something that must be considered when developing a data breach notification rule, however, or law is what will consumers be expected to do with that information. Do they just get a letter in the mail saying that their data was compromised and they are on their own? Or is there some recourse that the business or the corporation that had the data and then had it breached must provide to the consumer because the data was compromised?

Senator SCOTT. So not simply a uniformity across the Nation, but also some teeth as it relates to what happens next once the consumer is informed.

Mr. JAIKARAN. We see that across State laws now, where some of them are just a simple notification and some of them are some relationship that the corporation must have with the breached consumer.

Senator SCOTT. Thank you.

Mr. Smith, despite the Federal Government also being breached pretty frequently, unfortunately, some have suggested that we nationalize the credit reporting agencies. Such a move would kill innovation, the same innovation that is opening up the market of 26 million credit-invisible Americans. I think Fannie and Freddie should consider new credit reporting models that take into account things like rent payment and utilities. Who would benefit the most from such a change, Mr. Smith?

Mr. SMITH. So use of information about rent and utility payments by Fannie and Freddie could expand access to mortgage credit for younger consumers, recent immigrants, consumers who are new to credit, and others without a traditional credit file. So the national credit bureaus are already able to collect this information from landlords and utilities and have built the systems necessary to do that. And as you know, the credit bureaus over the last 50 years have been successful in expanding access to credit to folks who previously may not have had that access.

But I think ultimately it is going to be Fannie's and Freddie's decision whether or not these utility and rent payments are actually predictive of the risk of default that they are trying to manage.

Senator SCOTT. We certainly understand that Freddie and Fannie will have to make their own decisions, but the question was who benefits from it, and it sounds like to me that the population that benefits the most are those folks who are disproportionately represented today in homeownership.

Mr. SMITH. Yeah, well, folks who are creditworthy but we cannot tell because they do not have traditional credit report information, specifically people who are new to credit, I think.

Senator SCOTT. So I think the number—Senator Brown, I know you were thinking about South Carolina when I was talking there. The number is about 16 percent of South Carolinians who are today credit-invisible would become credit-visible and would show the responsible pattern that would allow them to own a home.

Thank you. Thank you, sir.

Senator BROWN. Thanks, Senator Scott. And my State is 5 million out of 11.6 million, so it is mid- to high 40 percent also.

Senator SCOTT. Thank you.

Senator BROWN. Senator Cortez Masto.

Senator CORTEZ MASTO. Thank you. Gentlemen, thank you so much for the conversation.

Mr. Smith, I wanted to start with you. As you note in your testimony, the CFPB's supervision of credit bureaus relates primarily to the accurate furnishing and reporting of credit data, and the CFPB does not generally provide for in-house supervisors. However, in the wake of the Equifax breach, Director Cordray has indicated that the CFPB supervision teams may be assigned to reside at the Big Three nationwide consumer reporting bureaus and monitor cybersecurity and data protection practices. Wouldn't you agree that this is an important development?

Mr. SMITH. Well, so when you look at Director Cordray's comments, I think you are talking about his CNBC, or something, comments on television. He said initially that the CFPB does not have authority over data security, and it seems as though the folks on the panel agree with that. Whether there is an appropriate role for a supervisor for data security at the credit bureaus, we want to talk with you about that and come up with the best result for consumers. It may be that if there is such a role to be played, that the CFPB is not the best person for the role, or it could very well be that they are.

Senator CORTEZ MASTO. Thank you.

Mr. Rotenberg, do you think this would be helpful? And let me put this in context because prior to my role here, I spent the last 8 years as Attorney General of Nevada. Nevada had one of the highest identity theft rates in the country, and I can tell you the breach that happened with Equifax is not equal to the breach that happened at a Target store or somewhere else. What happened with Equifax is now there is the potential of millions of Americans' identities being stolen. And if you have ever been the victim of identity theft, the rest of your life you are trying to reclaim your identity. And it is not just clearing up your credit. It is addressing somebody who has purchased a boat in your name, purchased a house in your name, committed a crime in your name when you are showing up in court and trying to identify that that person who committed a crime has stolen your identity. This is lifelong, and it is going to have a major impact on millions of Americans, and that is why this is so egregious. And we have to do a better job of protecting individuals' data and information because you are collecting it without their approval, and then they have to succumb to years of trying to clear up all of that data.

So my concern now is: How do we address it? How do we put limits on the data we collect? I know we are talking about more cybersecurity protection and making sure there is oversight over the companies. But if there is human error, or whatever occurred, it is going to happen again.

So is there some limit to the data that we should be collecting besides all of the other discussion that we talked about today? And so, Mr. Rotenberg, I am curious, your thoughts on that.

Mr. ROTENBERG. Well, Senator, to your first point, I think it would be a step in the right direction to have supervisory authority through CFPB at the credit reporting agencies. I think that makes a lot of sense. But, of course, that is only to prevent against future data breaches, and the question is what to do now for American consumers who confront the reality that others are in possession— we call these the "authenticators." This is the information that is used to establish your identity in commercial transactions. And this is the reason that we think we need to change the default on credit freezes. People should know from this point going forward anytime anyone wants access to their credit report. And people should know from this time going forward anytime there is suspicious activity on their credit reporting account. They should not have to select this service or pay for this service.

Senator CORTEZ MASTO. And I absolutely agree.

Mr. ROTENBERG. It should be built into the industry.

Senator CORTEZ MASTO. And I am going to cut you off, and I apologize because I only have so much time. I absolutely agree, and because there has been talk about uses of the Social Security number and limiting it in the private use, but I do not know about you, but when you go to set up your house and you set up your utilities, they ask for your Social Security number. When you go to your doctor's office, they ask for your Social Security number. This number has become so prevalent as an identifier, I do not know how you pull it back from the private sector. And, quite honestly, I do not know how you protect against anybody having access to it, because

I can tell you a bad guy is going to be able to go online, and if it has already been used and out there, they are going to find it.

So, more importantly for my purpose and I think all of our purposes, really shouldn't it be now giving the consumer the absolute right to control their information and how it is being used?

Mr. ROTENBERG. Absolutely, Senator, I think that is key. But if I could say briefly on the Social Security number, we have actually made some progress limiting its use. In fact, with credit to Senator Collins and Senator McCaskill, the Social Security number is now coming off the medical benefits ID card because its use there was contributing to identity theft among American seniors. We helped get the Social Security number off the State driver's license. The Social Security number is no longer published in the State voter rolls.

So this is an issue that can be addressed, but Congress will have to get behind an initiative that says to the private sector we have to limit the use of the SSN.

Senator CORTEZ MASTO. Thank you. I appreciate the comments. I notice my time is up. Thank you.

Chairman CRAPO [presiding]. Senator Kennedy.

Senator KENNEDY. Thank you, Mr. Chairman.

Gentlemen, I am sorry I missed your presentations. Why should we not pass legislation that would establish that the bureaus have a fiduciary obligation to the people whose data they collect and earn a profit off of?

Mr. ROTENBERG. Well, I think you should, Senator. I think some of that legislation is already in place with the Gramm–Leach–Bliley Act, but I think more needs to be done. And I think your description of a fiduciary relationship is absolutely correct.

Senator KENNEDY. Do you think there is a fiduciary relationship now?

Mr. ROTENBERG. No, I do not. I do not think the companies feel that they have an obligation to American consumers, and I think——

Senator KENNEDY. Do you gentlemen agree with that? I am sorry to cut you off.

Mr. SMITH. No, I disagree with that. No, I would not characterize it——

Senator KENNEDY. You disagree with that?

Mr. SMITH. ——as a fiduciary duty.

Senator KENNEDY. I am sorry. You disagree or agree?

Mr. SMITH. I disagree. I would not——

Senator KENNEDY. And you represent the bureaus——

Mr. SMITH. We represent the industry. We are subject to a pervasive regulatory scheme in this statute here, the Fair Credit Reporting Act, that requires us to ensure the accuracy of information in credit reports that requires us to——

Senator KENNEDY. Were you and your clients attempting—when the Equifax breach was made public, weren't you trying to pass legislation that would lessen your clients' liability?

Mr. SMITH. There was legislation that had been introduced that would introduce a cap on potential liability for private actions. That cap, though, would have been——

Senator KENNEDY. Do you think that was a good idea?

Mr. SMITH. The FCRA is unique among consumer credit protection statutes in that it does not have a cap on class action liability. So Truth in Lending, Equal Credit Opportunity, Fair Debt Collection, EFTA—all of these have caps. FCRA does not. The effort here——

Senator KENNEDY. Do you still believe your client should have caps, counselor?

Mr. SMITH. As a trade association, we would continue to argue for caps on——

Senator KENNEDY. Is that a "yes"?

Mr. SMITH. That is a "yes."

Senator KENNEDY. OK. Well, here is my problem. If the bureaus do their jobs right, they facilitate commerce, because when lenders loan money to people, the lenders want to get paid back. And what your clients offer is one assessment of the risk that the lenders are taking. It is just one assessment. There are others who do not use online lending. Many online lenders do not use your clients' product anymore. They think there are other ways, better ways to assess risk. I am not saying they are right or wrong. I am saying that your clients basically take my data, personal information about me, without my permission; and as a business model, they sell it to businesses. I am not compensated.

Now, if they lose my data, as Equifax did, or if someone submits to them data that is in error that undermines my credit score, the bureaus have no obligation or interest right now to work with me to try to get the credit score correct.

Have you ever had one of the bureaus get your credit score wrong and you called and tried to get it fixed? Have any of you?

Mr. JAIKARAN. No, I have not, Senator.

Mr. ROTENBERG. No, Senator.

Senator KENNEDY. Well, it is not an easy process. And it would seem to me that—I am not trying to undermine the bureaus, but it seems to me, first of all, that you could develop technology very easily that would allow people to go to an app on their phone to put a credit freeze on and off free of charge. That ought to be a minimum.

Number two, you need to explain to the American people how you are protecting their data on which your clients are making a profit. Most of the adults in Louisiana had their data stolen by Equifax. And they had to go to a lot of trouble to go freeze credit. Some of them are going to have their identities stolen. And it is just not right. It is just not right. And we are looking to you gentlemen to tell us what to do about it. And, counselor, I do not mean to pick on you, and I understand you are representing your clients, but your clients need to step up to the plate here and suggest some meaningful reforms, or some reforms are going to be suggested to them.

Mr. SMITH. Right. Well——

Senator KENNEDY. And my advice to you would be to step up to the plate and offer specific things that you and your clients are going to do to improve this situation, not platitudes, not bromides, specific suggestions.

Mr. SMITH. Right.

Senator KENNEDY. Because a lot of Americans did not know what a credit bureau was. They know now.

I went over. I am sorry, Mr. Chairman.

Chairman CRAPO. Thank you.

Senator Warren.

Senator WARREN. Thank you, Mr. Chairman.

So at the hearing 2 weeks ago with the former CEO of Equifax, there was a lot of agreement between Democrats and Republicans that consumers should be able to control their own data, and without consumer control, credit reporting companies really have no reason to treat us well. We are not their customers. We are just their products. And it shows.

A 2012 study by the Federal Trade Commission found that one out of every five people had an error in their credit reports. Meanwhile, over last year the Consumer Financial Protection Bureau has fielded hundreds of thousands of consumer complaints. And the Big Three credit reporting agencies are now the three most complained about companies in the entire financial services industry.

You know, if you ran a restaurant and got your customers' orders wrong 20 percent of the time and had the worst customer service in town, you would be out of business in a week. But credit reporting companies, not them. They are getting bigger, they are getting richer, and they are getting more powerful. This market is clearly broken, and fixing it starts with giving customers more control over their own data.

So, Mr. Rotenberg, I have introduced the FREE Act with Senator Schatz and more than a dozen other Senators. Our bill would let every consumer freeze and unfreeze access to their credit files for free.

So I want to ask: Do you think that would be a good idea to give consumers more control over their data?

Mr. ROTENBERG. Senator Warren, I think it is an excellent proposal, and as you say, I think the key to this industry is giving consumers greater control over the use of their personal data. It begins by moving to an opt-in model, allowing the consumer to decide in which circumstances it is in their interest for their credit report to be released to someone else.

Senator WARREN. Thank you. You know, companies like Equifax do more than issue credit reports. They also sell your information to businesses that want to sell something in turn back to the customer. Our bill also makes clear that no credit reporting agency can sell your data if your credit file is frozen. Other legislative proposals and the new lock that Equifax is rolling out right now do not give customers that right.

So let me ask this part: Do you think that consumers should have the right to freeze the data so that it stops a credit reporting agency from selling access to the consumer's data?

Mr. ROTENBERG. Absolutely, Senator. The model does not work unless consumers maintain control, and so many problems of the industry result from the industry pushing the burdens back onto the consumers to choose the freeze, to choose the monitoring service, to inspect their credit reports. It is entirely upside down, and it is the reason that we have record levels of identity theft today in the U.S.

Senator WARREN. Thank you. I think that is a powerful point. You know, if companies like Equifax do not pay us to sell our information to other people, then we should not have to pay them to stop selling it.

According to your testimony, you were saying—and I think you mentioned this earlier, Mr. Rotenberg—you would go even further. You would make the default position that a consumer's account is frozen until the credit reporting agency gets the consumer's explicit permission to unfreeze the account to share the data. In other words, consumers would have to opt into sharing their data rather than opt out. What is the reason for that?

Mr. ROTENBERG. Senator, I think it is just common sense. No one is objecting to the provision of credit to American consumers. It is obviously critical for our economy, makes it possible for people to purchase homes and cars and even cell phones. But it is the consumer who is initiating the commercial transaction; it is the consumer who is seeking the mortgage or the loan. The consumer should decide when to release that credit record information to others, and they should know, by the way, what information is contained in the credit report. They may be wrongfully denied a loan from a bank that the bank would provide but for the fact that the credit reporting agency has provided inaccurate information.

Senator WARREN. All right. So powerfully important that we be able to protect our own privacy, that we be able to make sure that it is accurate. In your testimony, though, you raised one more point. You say we need to fix the credit reporting industry in order to protect our national security. I am about out of time, but could you just say a word about that?

Mr. ROTENBERG. Very briefly, Senator, I mentioned earlier that when the Fair Credit Reporting Act was passed in 1970, the concern was the misuse of personal data by the credit reporting agency. That concern remains. But what has changed now almost 50 years later is that data is now the target of foreign adversaries, and we have to realistically consider that the people who get access to our personal data held by these companies have interests adverse to our Nation. That is an additional reason to strengthen these privacy laws.

Senator WARREN. Thank you very much. You know, the credit reporting agency is a threat to each of us personally, but it is also a threat to our national security. We need to give consumers more control over their data, need to reform this industry, and that is what we are trying to do with the FREE Act. Thank you very much.

Thank you, Mr. Chairman.

Chairman CRAPO. Thank you.

Senator Tillis.

Senator TILLIS. Thank you, Mr. Chairman. Gentlemen, thank you for being here.

One question that I have, when you have something like the breach at Equifax, Congress has never seen a legitimate problem that needs to be dealt with, an opportunity to overreact. And so one of the things that I am concerned with is when we have this discussion—I want to start with something simple, and then maybe I can build on things to the extent time allows. But when we had the Equifax CEO in here, I tried to ask him the question of the lock—they are calling it "Lock for Life"—versus delete.

Mr. Rotenberg, where are you on the option of the consumer being able to delete any presence of their existence in any of the Big Three credit reporting agencies? Do you think that is something they should be entitled to do?

Mr. ROTENBERG. Well, I do, Senator. In fact, this country has a long tradition of expungement of financial records to give people the opportunity to start over, even after bankruptcy. So we have already recognized that people should be given the opportunity to, you know, reapply for credit, even after they have had those type of experiences.

Senator TILLIS. So if they delete it and then later they were seeking credit and they had no reliable sources for showing creditworthiness, who is it on to provide all the information that may be needed to underwrite a loan or get a credit card or some other financial instrument? Anybody on the panel is welcome to opine——

Mr. ROTENBERG. Well, I would just say in those circumstances, of course, the absence of the background information could well be a factor in the credit determination. But that is not a reason not to give the consumer the opportunity to delete the data if the consumer chooses to do so.

Senator TILLIS. But at the end of the day, the consumer needs to be fully aware it could be on them to actually produce information that could be used as a basis to underwrite—the absence of information would likely result in no credit being extended.

Mr. SMITH. Here is another concern, Senator. What happens if the consumer selectively deletes information? So I have three credit cards, and I have decided that I am not going to pay one of them, and I delete that trade line from my file. How will a bank be able to manage that credit risk if consumers can delete accurate and relevant information?

And with respect to this fresh start idea, the FCRA already allows for that. Any information that is derogatory in your credit record comes off after 7 years.

Senator TILLIS. I think one thing that—when we discussed this with the breach, I think one thing that the credit reporting agencies need to demonstrate is that they do not make their problem the consumer's problem. In other words, if you have a breach, then you should be treating that consumer like you will move heaven and earth to clear up the problem. It should not be something that requires months of paperwork and hours of their time to clean up, if, in fact, you can point it back to the breach, and that is something I will be interested in seeing how Equifax handles it.

But I am concerned, Mr. Rotenberg, with the idea of just the aggregation of data that is used to predict how cohorts may, you know, behave in terms of creditworthiness, that if we continue to reduce the base, do you think there is any threat to the fact that we have less reliable information to move capital or to provide resources to people who need it?

Mr. ROTENBERG. I think it is important for businesses to have access to relevant and accurate consumer data. I think they should be accountable and transparent about how that data is being used.

Senator TILLIS. Would you consider then the selective deletion of credit data as being accurate and relevant data for the financial services industry?

Mr. ROTENBERG. It may or may not be. I mean, the credit decision is based on a wide variety of factors, many of which, by the way, are not even known to consumers. So we do not know how they are making determinations about us, yet they are concerned if they do not know everything about us when they make their decisions. And that just seems a little unfair.

Senator TILLIS. One other in my remaining time. I was not here, but I think someone else answered the question. But what do you think is the—what technologies or maybe what processes out there are we using to get away from Social Security numbers as authentication methods and moving more to say what the card industry has done with tokenization, trying to come up with some sort of an identity that will actually eliminate or substantially reduce what is a relatively easy thing to do, and that is, to get somebody's indicative information and commit fraud? I mean, what is out there that we should be looking at and as a matter of public policy should be promoting? Go right down the line, and my time is expired after this answer.

Mr. JAIKARAN. I am sorry, Senator. I am not aware of any particular token products that could be used. One point to know with the use of technology, though, is that there may be people in the sample size, citizens, consumers, that do not have access to something like a cell phone, so they would be barred from participating in the widespread use of technology, and that is one consideration to make when establishing public policy.

Mr. ROTENBERG. I think as a general matter, if we have distributed and contextualized identity, in other words, the company learns only what it needs to learn to make a decision, that is the best approach. Today we are at the opposite end of the spectrum with an open-ended identifier that makes it possible for companies to learn just about anything they want to about an individual.

Mr. SMITH. So I think that if we did not have the Social, we would need to invent it. So if we take away the Social, we will need to come up with another unique identifier.

As I said earlier, with a name like Andrew Smith, it is critically important that people are able to distinguish between the thousands or tens of thousands of individuals named Andrew Smith just simply to identify which one are you—not necessarily to authenticate that I am indeed who I say I am, but just which one are you. And the Social plays a critical role there. And if not the Social, then we need something else to fill that role.

Senator TILLIS. Thank you.

Chairman CRAPO. Thank you.

Senator Schatz.

Senator SCHATZ. Thank you, Mr. Chairman.

Mr. Smith, after the Equifax breach, consumers learned that the best way to protect themselves from identity theft and fraud was to freeze their credit report. But when they went to do that, they found a complicated process that required contacting each of the three credit bureaus, generating and remembering separate PINs for each and, most infuriating, paying 10 bucks to each bureau to

place the freeze, not to mention the fees that they have to incur
if they want to lift the freeze later. Equifax's lapse in data security
will be rewarded by hundreds of millions of dollars in revenue to
the company that made the mistake.

And so my question for you is very simple: Explain to me why
Equifax, Experian, and TransUnion charge people to freeze their
credit report when there is a mistake that is their fault.

Mr. SMITH. Well, so there are a lot of ways for consumers to protect themselves, and for certain consumers freezes are the right
choice. I personally——

Senator SCHATZ. And so in those—hold on.

Mr. SMITH. OK.

Senator SCHATZ. In those instances why is it not free? If the consumer——

Mr. SMITH. Right now we have—as you know, right now we have
a patchwork of laws, and if we are to have a single national standard, I think that, you know, we would be happy to talk with you
about how to get that result right for consumers. But it——

Senator SCHATZ. Well, what has that got to do with—a patchwork of laws, what has that got to do with anything? I am asking——

Mr. SMITH. Because the patchwork——

Senator SCHATZ. Hold on.

Mr. SMITH. Right.

Senator SCHATZ. I am asking you when a mistake occurs and 144
million people are told to do a certain thing, that certain thing
should be free, shouldn't it?

Mr. SMITH. I do not know that everyone was told to freeze their
credit report. Personally, I do not think it is the right choice for everyone. I do think that the credit bureaus make the freeze——

Senator SCHATZ. But it is the right choice for some number of
millions of Americans, is it not?

Mr. SMITH. I believe that all three of the nationwide credit bureaus make freezes available for free to individuals who say that
they are identity theft victims. I believe that they also make
freezes available for free to senior citizens and to minors.

As far as a national freeze requirement, I think that we
would——

Senator SCHATZ. I am not asking you about a requirement. I am
asking you why you generate revenue off of the mistakes of the organizations that you represent.

Mr. SMITH. Well, the why is because freezes cost money, and also
the State laws——

Senator SCHATZ. But the locks are free, right?

Mr. SMITH. ——permit a charge—locks, I do not know from, I am
afraid. I saw the testimony from the CEO of Equifax——

Senator SCHATZ. You are the counsel for this organization.

Mr. SMITH. These are new products—I am a counsel for the trade
association, but I know that there are all kinds of new products
that credit bureaus and others are rolling out that can take advantage of, for example, apps on a mobile device and lock and unlock.
But I do not know that those—any of those products are necessarily in the market now.

Senator SCHATZ. I do not understand what you are saying, and I do not think that it is because I do not understand this area. I think it is because I do not understand what you are saying because at a common-sense level—I want you to try to explain to somebody you went to high school with—right?—who says, "Oh, you got a gig with the CRAs. Good for you. How is that going? Let me ask you a question, Andrew. Why do I have to pay for a freeze?" And I do not think you answered that question.

Mr. SMITH. And the answer is because freezes cost money. Freezes have to be implemented by the credit bureaus.

Senator SCHATZ. Then the question is: Why did the company that made the mistake make a profit off of that mistake? Why are you charging consumers? Even if the freezes cost money, fine, you should eat it because that would create an incentive to not screw up again.

Mr. SMITH. I thought Equifax was providing freezes for free.

Senator SCHATZ. But my question is: Why not all three, and why not as a matter of course? And that only occurred after the CEO quit and under great pressure.

Mr. SMITH. I thought they offered freezes for free right up front.

Senator SCHATZ. No. I want to ask you a couple of questions related to a bill that I have introduced. Do you think it is a good idea for credit bureaus to use tighter matching requirements so that the trade lines on someone's credit report are more likely to be their own information?

Mr. SMITH. I think that matching algorithms are a really tricky issue, as I am sure you have done some thinking about it, and it is really a question of probabilities and statistics, and I am not sure that we necessarily want to legislate that. But matching is critically important for accuracy.

Senator SCHATZ. And what is your error rate, roughly?

Mr. SMITH. We believe that our error rate—so the FTC did a study, of course, as you know, in 2012. We did a similar study, and we believe that the error rate from our study is less than 1 percent. Looking at the FTC's study, we believe—and this is in an appendix to the FTC's study. Based on the FTC's data, we believe that the error rate is about 2 percent.

Now, error is an important concept here, though. It has to be an error that moves the needle, that would have an effect on the consumer. So they get my date of birth wrong. That is not necessarily an error if it does not move the needle on my credit score.

Senator SCHATZ. So you are talking about even at the low end—even at the low end of the estimate, you are talking about a million, 2 million individuals who have——

Mr. SMITH. Absolutely, and that is not acceptable. And I think that——

Senator SCHATZ. And whose responsibility is that?

Mr. SMITH. Well, it is a lot of people's responsibility, but it is to some extent the credit bureaus' responsibility. And as far as accuracy is concerned, accuracy—Professor Rotenberg in his written testimony said that, look, you are never going to have perfect data security, there are always going to be breaches; the best we can do is to try to control them up front.

Accuracy is the same way. It is a process.

Senator SCHATZ. I am over time. I will just add that I understand that you are going to make mistakes. The basic question is: Who should incur the costs of those mistakes—you guys or the rest of the country?

Thank you.

Chairman CRAPO. Senator Perdue.

Senator PERDUE. Thank you, Chair. Thank you, guys, for being here. It is a very complicated conversation.

Let me start with something we are working on to codify something across 47 States. Right now, if you want to, you have to opt out, basically. In other words, I never gave permission to anybody to get that data, although it does provide a service so that I do not have to aggregate all my credit information when I want to go borrow something. So I get that. But at the Equifax breach hearing I think just 2 weeks ago, we asked questions regarding the need for a national standard on credit freezes, and I think Representative McHenry has already—he has the PROTECT Act that you may be familiar with that they are proposing. It creates a national standard for credit freezes, harmonizing the current 47 State laws on the issue.

I would like to get all three of you to comment. Do you agree that that would help allow the development of technology such as apps that could freeze and unfreeze without having to go through the process and so somebody could actually open up, get the credit information they need, and then opt out easily, without having to have a lot of instruction? Is that something that might benefit us here?

Mr. SMITH. So as I said earlier, freezes are not the right choice for everybody necessarily, but they are the right choice for some people, and, you know, the development of a national standard is something that we would welcome.

With respect to this lock and unlock functionality, I would ask you to consider that whenever we legislate something like this, the questions that come up say, "Well, what about the people who do not have smartphones? What are we going to do about them?"

"Well, OK, we are going to have a lock and unlock functionality where you dial an 800 number. Well, what about the people who do not have easy access to a telephone? Well, we will have a mail-in."

Senator PERDUE. But they would not be—just so I am clear, they would not be in the system—in other words, I could not access their data unless they——

Mr. SMITH. Flipped the switch.

Senator PERDUE. Unless they were to come back and do something like this, on an 800 number or whatever, when they needed it.

Mr. SMITH. Correct. But then you think to yourself, OK, let us do an 800 number. Well, that is going to present a security risk that someone else unlocks my credit when they are applying for an auto loan on a Saturday afternoon. So that means a PIN. So I do not know what my PIN is, I have forgotten it. Well, then you are going to have to reset your PIN. And before you know it, you are not going to get that new cell phone at the Verizon store on a Saturday afternoon. You are going to have to go reset your PIN. You are going to have to go back to the Verizon store the next weekend, and hopefully it will work out.

But, see, there is a lot of friction in the system, and these freezes and locks are difficult to administer, and that is why they are not necessarily the right choice for everybody. But for some people who are not credit active, who are not buying cell phones or renting apartments.

Mr. ROTENBERG. Senator, I actually think it is a good proposal, and I think it is a step in the right direction. I am, frankly, a little confused by Mr. Smith's comments. Most of what he is describing are the difficulties that the industry has created in giving consumers the ability to select the freeze, to limit the access by others. And what the legislation I think would accomplish is to simplify that process, make it easier for people to make those decisions precisely so they can have the credit record information available when they need it to be made available.

Mr. JAIKARAN. Regarding any congressional action in this space, it is an interesting public policy question, because there are these groups of data brokers who have this information and they have their business relationships with those that they acquire information from and those that they sell the information to. However, the information is the consumer's. And the relationship between the data broker and the consumer is a little weaker compared to who they are selling data to and who they are acquiring it from. The weakness in that link is a space where Federal policy may be able to bridge the gap between the rights of the consumer and the rights of the data broker, or the right of the data broker relative to the consumer of their own data.

Senator PERDUE. All right. Thank you. Let us talk about Social Security numbers for a minute, if I may. The same thing. Adoption of Social Security numbers as a method goes back, I think, to the 1960s. But in the last half-century, our technology has moved fairly rapidly forward. Is there a better way? The new technologies we have in front of us, isn't there a better, more secure way to matching people with accounts such as tokenization, or should all of these cyberattacks with—and should all these cyberattacks be the impetus to start planning out what transition to credit future without Social Security numbers? Social Security numbers seem to me to be the Holy Grail here that is the access beyond what any reasonable person would want. Is that a reasonable direction?

Mr. ROTENBERG. Senator, I think the key here is to limit the use of the SSN but not replace it. In other words, it is the weak link in the information industry. It is the target of identity thieves. And if you are trying to make your industry more resilient against those attacks, you have to reduce your dependency on the SSN. But, you see, if you replace the SSN with another general purpose identifier, that becomes the target. So we need a more distributed approach to identification, not a single point of failure. That is what the SSN has become.

Senator PERDUE. Well, it is pretty obvious to me we have got to engage on this, but we do not have a common answer yet to this security issue. Thank you. I am out of time.

Thank you, Mr. Chair.

Chairman CRAPO. Senator Heitkamp.

Senator HEITKAMP. Thank you, Mr. Chairman.

Not to extend the discussion on when you can put a credit freeze on or put a lock on, it is interesting you said you can—Mr. Smith, you said you can put a lock on after you have been a victim of identity theft. That is kind of like saying, you know, lock the door after the thief went in your house. I mean, it is just not—it is not responsive to what we are trying to get at here, which is we understand the benefit of an aggregator of data that gives us easier access to credit. I think no one is disagreeing with that.

The question is—and you were asked about fiduciary obligations, and the question really is: What responsibility does that aggregator have when something like this happens?

Now, when Mr. Smith was here, the previous Mr. Smith, Equifax——

Mr. SMITH. No relation.

Senator HEITKAMP. Yeah, I figured that. He said, "This happens all the time. You know, we are hit all the time." And I asked, "Well, in light of that, then why did you seem so ill prepared when you were actually breached? Why did it take you so long to come up with a response to the breach?"

So I have got a series of questions on: How often does this happen? And what is the general response that the industry has? So as a general matter, how many times per year on average would a company like Equifax, TransUnion, or Experian experience—how often would you experience a breach that would be reported to the FBI?

Mr. SMITH. So, unfortunately, I do not have those figures. We can find them. I would say that, based on my personal knowledge, none of the credit bureaus themselves have been breached. Now, the companies—in Equifax's case, it was information that was outside of the consumer reporting agency data base. We also know of a breach at Experian involving data of T–Mobile. So there are breaches that occur, and we will come up with a number for how frequently they occur. But to the best of my knowledge, there has never been a security breach of a consumer reporting agency data base.

Senator HEITKAMP. And that is splitting a hair for the consumers. I do not think there is any doubt about it.

Mr. SMITH. Well, but it is an important policy point, I think, because if the FTC and CFPB after their investigations conclude that the consumer reporting agency data base was not breached, after Equifax was subjected to this punishing attack, that might inform our policy choices.

Senator HEITKAMP. The next question I have is: Let us say that you report it to the FBI. What is the typical guidelines or strategies that any of these credit agencies, any of them would basically go to? Do you have like a fire drill, in other words? Do you have a system in place that will lock down and protect data?

Mr. SMITH. Right. So now, of course, I cannot speak for any particular company, but the companies with which I am familiar have incident response plans, and they have done the table—they call it a "tabletop exercise" where, you know, all the stakeholders are around the table and we run through, you know: What is the public statement going to be? What are we going to do with respect to our call centers? How do we inform law enforcement? How are we going to do the consumer notifications? That kind of stuff.

Senator HEITKAMP. You know, but you would have to agree that Equifax was pretty ill prepared.

Mr. SMITH. I do not know. I think this was an unprecedented breach. So I would rather not speak to——

Senator HEITKAMP. Even if it is 10 people, the response should be the same as if it were 140 million people.

Mr. SMITH. Well, except think about your call center, for example. So rather than ten calls—ten calls you can handle. A hundred and forty million on 1 day?

Senator HEITKAMP. Well, doesn't that beg the question of why people here are upset? I mean, you had Senator Kennedy basically say, look, this is not data that you own. You do not have a relationship with the consumer other than an aggregator that provides that service. If I say, "I do not want your service, I will aggregate my own data, I will take responsibility," I have to pay you so that you are not collecting my data. Correct?

Mr. SMITH. Not collecting. This is a freeze, right? The data is still there, but you have frozen it, and you have the right to unfreeze it.

Senator HEITKAMP. You know, in Europe, all across the EU, there is a whole lot of privacy initiatives: the right to be forgotten—you know, we are getting close to that here. We have been a much more open economy as it relates to this kind of data aggregation. The more we do not see a response, the closer we are to that pendulum that Senator Tillis talked about, which is the potential that you guys are going to be out of business because every American is going to say, "We do not want your service."

Mr. SMITH. No; absolutely, we need to ensure that consumers and businesses trust the national credit reporting system——

Senator HEITKAMP. And I think you have a serious trust problem today. And I think the lack of coming forth with solutions and the adversarial kind of approach that we have seen to this is not helping to solve the problem. So we look forward to ongoing discussions.

Mr. SMITH. As do we.

Senator HEITKAMP. Thank you, Mr. Smith.

Chairman CRAPO. Thank you.

Senator Donnelly.

Senator DONNELLY. Thank you, Mr. Chairman. Thank you, panelists.

Mr. Smith—or this is actually to all of you. In 2014, the Department of Veterans Affairs created the Choice Program to allow vets to receive medical care in non-VA facilities. It has been helpful in increasing access. However, issues with the implementation of the program led to delayed payments and billing problems, which in turn resulted in some vets receiving adverse actions on their credit reports from debt collection efforts. Adverse credit actions make it more difficult and expensive for them to get a mortgage, to buy a car, and it is really troubling that our veterans have had their credit harmed through no fault of their own.

Senator Rounds and I introduced the Protecting Veterans' Credit Act to delay the reporting of VA-responsible medical debt, to make it easier for this erroneous debt to be removed from credit reports.

Mr. Smith, medical debt can obviously get expensive. What damage can it do to the vet's credit when this is reported as unpaid?

Mr. SMITH. Well, look, we agree with you 100 percent that veterans should not have their credit records tarnished by backlogs and inefficiencies in VA's payment system, and we understand that that is what is happening here, and we are committed to working with you to solve that issue through the national credit reporting system. I think institutionally we believe that the folks who are best able to solve that issue are the VA and the private medical service providers and the debt collectors who are furnishing this essentially erroneous information into the system. But we are committed to working with you and your office.

Senator DONNELLY. So I have your commitment on behalf of the trade association, on behalf of the industry, that you will work together with us to address these problems, to address the difficulty of the reporting of VA-related medical debt that our vets will not get dinged on their credit reports for this occurring?

Mr. SMITH. Right. For erroneous, right? What we are talking about is where VA, because of VA's processing inefficiencies, they just have not paid the bill——

Senator DONNELLY. Well, it is not erroneous that my knee got worked on. It is erroneous that the bill came to me as a veteran, if I was a vet.

Mr. SMITH. Correct, and VA should have paid it, and the private medical service provider has not been paid and furnishes the information, yeah, we need to fix that. And we are committed to working with you to fix that.

Senator DONNELLY. OK. Congress enacted the Fair Credit Reporting Act in 1970 to set the rules of the road. Despite the original act and the many subsequent amendments, we still do not control our information contained in the files of the credit bureaus. It is reported without any consumer permission, as has been noted by many. It is often sold to third parties, such as with pre-screened credit and insurance offers. And the personal information may now be available to thieves on the Dark Web after Equifax.

Mr. Smith, you are the representative for the association. Should consumers have more control over their information?

Mr. SMITH. Well, so we have talked a little bit about that today, you know, the ability to remove yourself from the system, the ability to selectively delete information. I think both of those present issues for the national credit reporting system. The selective deletion would allow a consumer to game the system, to hide unpaid debts from potential creditors, making it—presenting a real concern for the safety and soundness.

Senator DONNELLY. Well, that comes out if they apply for something, right? If they want to get a mortgage, then the mortgage company——

Mr. SMITH. Well, I am talking about the selective deletion. Now, the removal from the system, then the removal from the system is great until you need to rent an apartment or buy a cell phone or get a mortgage or get a car loan, and then there is nothing——

Senator DONNELLY. Then you can opt in, right?

Mr. SMITH. Well, not if your information has been removed from the system. If it is removed, it is removed.

Now, what you are talking about is perhaps a freeze, and I think we are—we think that a freeze is the right choice for some consumers, not for all consumers, and that we are willing to work with——

Senator DONNELLY. Well, isn't it appropriate that the consumer ought to be able to make that decision? If it makes it a little bit harder for them to get the apartment, that is a decision they have made. Mr. Rotenberg.

Mr. ROTENBERG. Absolutely, Senator, and I think it is important to understand that if a consumer is making a significant decision like renting an apartment or applying for a home mortgage or a car loan, it makes sense to have them have the ability to know what is in the credit report and make the affirmative decision to decide who is going to get access to that information. So that would be common sense.

Senator DONNELLY. Thank you, Mr. Chairman.

Chairman CRAPO. Thank you.

Senator Van Hollen.

Senator VAN HOLLEN. Thank you, Mr. Chairman. And I thank all of you for being here today.

It does seem, as reflected in a lot of the comments today and from the earlier hearings we had, that the credit reporting agency model is one that is in some ways uniquely stacked against consumers when there has been either a data breach or bad data put in. And my question goes beyond the issue of the data breach to lots of complaints we have heard over the years about credit reporting agencies collecting bad data that then goes to lead to a denial of a loan or a mortgage payment. And there has been a lot of discussion about how to sort of allow that consumer to be made whole.

My question is on the front end in terms of creating penalties or deterrents for those who are collecting all this data without people's permission and then having the burden be on the consumer on the other side.

So my question to all of you is: Is there some kind of deterrent that we could put in place so that the burden and the penalty for collecting and disseminating bad data, whether it is through a breach or whether it is through denial of a credit card can actually address this problem on the front end so that there is more of a premium for a credit reporting agency to prevent that from happening in the first place?

Mr. SMITH. So I would like to start in responding to that. So with respect to data accuracy, credit bureaus have substantial duties with respect to data accuracy, and those are up front to ensure that they have procedures in place to ensure the maximum possible accuracy of the data. The companies that furnish data into the credit bureaus are now required to have written policies and procedures to ensure the accuracy of that data. So that is up front. And the credit bureaus and the people who furnish the data into the credit bureaus are all supervised for adherence to those standards by the Consumer Financial Protection Bureau right now. So I think that— so we do have—I mean, we are not unregulated. We do have this statute, and it gets longer every year. And there are more and more duties added in for credit bureaus and furnishers——

Senator VAN HOLLEN. So I guess my question is: What is the current penalty in the event that bad data gets in? Despite all of the systems that are put in place, is there a penalty that has to be paid by the credit reporting agencies? I am not talking about after the fact. In other words, in addition to just bringing the consumer whole—because let us say you are a consumer, right?

Mr. SMITH. Right.

Senator VAN HOLLEN. You know, you get denied a loan. Then you have got to go through the incredible hassle of getting all this straightened out. And at the end of the day, OK, maybe you get your loan. But what can we do to put more of a deterrent up front so that we never get to that point where thousands of people are wrongfully denied a loan, and, you know, after a whole lot of work and cost, maybe they get the loan? So I am interested in your thoughts, and then I may come back——

Mr. ROTENBERG. Let me say, Senator, right now I think it is upside down. In other words, right now, when there is a problem, the companies turn around and charge the consumers to take advantage of the tools they need to correct the problem. So that cannot be right. I think what we do need to do is increase the incentives for the companies to do a better job on data security and on privacy protection.

If I could make one more historical point, there is a deal at the heart of the Fair Credit Reporting Act. When the FCRA was passed by Congress in 1970, the ability for consumers to bring suit in State tort law was preempted because it was their information and some of this inaccurate, incomplete, is disparaging and defamatory and causes commercial loss. Before passage of the FCRA, people could bring lawsuits for those harms. They cannot now under the FCRA, which means that Congress has to strengthen the penalties to maintain the incentives.

Senator VAN HOLLEN. Right. So there is a good example, right? If someone collects bad data that harms somebody, would you agree, Mr. Smith, that they should be able to have recourse through the courts?

Mr. SMITH. Well, they do have recourse, and the recourse is through this law. Now, remember that this law provides for statutory penalties in private actions where the credit bureau behaved willfully.

Senator VAN HOLLEN. Let me ask you, because my time may be running out here, your association has been lobbying against the Consumer Financial Protection Bureau's provision that would allow people to bring lawsuits. In other words, you have been lobbying in favor of keeping mandatory arbitration. Isn't that right?

Mr. SMITH. That is my understanding, that, yes, we are lobbying for that.

Senator VAN HOLLEN. Doesn't that stack the deck against the consumer? You mentioned 143 million people, right? If everybody has got to go to mandatory arbitration as opposed to being able to group together as consumers and bring a case, that definitely stacks the deck in favor of the big guys and against the person who has been harmed, doesn't it?

Mr. SMITH. But with respect to the credit reporting system, there is no opportunity—you have no contract with Equifax.

Senator VAN HOLLEN. I understand.

Mr. SMITH. So you have no mandatory arbitration clause with Equifax. Correct?

Senator VAN HOLLEN. But this is a separate issue actually that was just raised by another witness. In other words, if there is information in there that causes me damage—right?

Mr. SMITH. Information in the credit report you can——

Senator VAN HOLLEN. Yes, that causes me damage.

Mr. SMITH. You can sue, and you can be a member of a class because there is no mandatory arbitration clause in that context. What we are talking about with arbitration is where the consumer is purchasing a product from one of the credit bureaus, like a credit monitoring product, for example, and——

Senator VAN HOLLEN. But we did see in the case of Equifax, at least initially, that as a condition of getting protection from damaging information that Equifax breaches caused, that they were originally requiring people to relinquish their rights to go to court. In other words, they were insisting they sign something for mandatory arbitration.

Mr. SMITH. With respect to——

Senator VAN HOLLEN. Now, they backed—no, but this is an example——

Mr. SMITH. Then they backed off, correct.

Senator VAN HOLLEN. And there are other Equifax products where there is a contractual relationship where they are insisting on mandatory arbitration. Isn't that the case?

Mr. SMITH. For credit monitoring and——

Senator VAN HOLLEN. I mean, they testified here they have lots of products where they insist on——

Mr. SMITH. Yes, direct——

Senator VAN HOLLEN. Doesn't that——

Mr. SMITH. ——products sold to consumers, yes.

Senator VAN HOLLEN. And if a consumer is wronged in that process, doesn't it stack the deck against them to say they have to go through mandatory arbitration?

Mr. SMITH. Well, of course, I am going to disagree with that. I mean, we think that arbitration can be effective. We also think that given the statute called the "Credit Repair Organizations Act" that there are special risks presented for credit monitoring products that have stacked the deck against the company.

Senator VAN HOLLEN. I would just say, Mr. Chairman, I can understand why Equifax would want to deny that particular kind of recourse because it can be more successful in recovering people's damages. Thank you.

Chairman CRAPO. Thank you, Senator. And hold on 1 second.

[Pause.]

Chairman CRAPO. I am going to wrap it up. I am going to have to be very fast because there is a second vote that I am going to have to get to.

So thank you very much for attending here today. I just have one question, and I know that you are here as experts on credit bureaus. I just want to know, if you know, whether there is data that is required to be submitted by the credit bureaus to the Federal

Government. Does any Federal Government agency require credit bureaus to submit data to them?

Mr. SMITH. I do not believe that—so I know that data is provided to the Federal Reserve Board and to the CFPB by credit bureaus, and I believe that that data is purchased by those agencies and that it is provided within the strictures of the Fair Credit Reporting Act. And in the instances with which I am familiar, it is provided in a deidentified and an aggregated format.

Chairman CRAPO. All right. That does it then. I want to thank each——

Senator BROWN. Could I ask some more questions? Thank you. [Pause.]

Senator BROWN [presiding]. Then I will wrap up, right? OK. Thank you.

Mr. Rotenberg, let me start with you. If Americans could make CRAs delete their credit files upon demand, like the law requires for medical records—and I know you have some interesting thoughts there, but do not go into so much the medical records. But if they could delete their credit files upon demand, would that create an additional business risk for consumer reporting agencies?

Mr. ROTENBERG. Well, I do not know if it would create a risk for consumer reporting agencies. It would give consumers more control of their personal information, and I think there is a way to manage that. Certainly it is done currently with bankruptcy and the FCRA.

Senator BROWN. Would you say that consumer reporting agencies would not want Americans to demand that their credit files be deleted?

Mr. ROTENBERG. I am certain or I expect that would be their position. They try to get as much information about consumers as they can, and, of course, consumers have very little information about what is being gathered.

Senator BROWN. Let me make sure I understand. So if CRAs knew that Americans would request their data be deleted after a cybersecurity breach like we just had, and they unsuccessfully tried to do that following the Equifax breach, as we also know, would that create an incentive for these agencies to pay more attention to cybersecurity in the first place?

Mr. ROTENBERG. I am sure it would, and I think to answer your question directly, consumer reporting agencies have no legal right to obtain the information of American consumers. The businesses have evolved over time. They have collected a lot of data. They are subject to regulation. But I do not think the credit reporting agencies can claim that they have any right to access our personal data, and so ultimately it would be the consumer's decision whether or not any company has the right to possess our data.

Senator BROWN. So some at the CRAs claim that consumers would game the system. Is that right?

Mr. ROTENBERG. Well, it is possible. But, you know, of course, right now I think the credit reporting agencies largely game the system because consumers do not know the factors that are used to make decisions about them for credit, for employment, and even for cell phone purchases. So it is very asymmetric, this industry, who has information about who and how that information is used.

Senator BROWN. Speaking of asymmetric, currently my understanding is that rules for privacy are much stricter at Government agencies than they are in the private sector. If that is the case—and I think it is—should we consider a single set of privacy standards for both public and private?

Mr. ROTENBERG. I think that is the unfinished business of privacy protection in the United States. We had a moment where there was an opportunity to establish a comprehensive privacy law in the private sector. Congress chose not to. There is a comprehensive law for Federal agencies.

Europe took a different approach. They established comprehensive privacy protection for the private sector, and I think there has been some benefit. They do not face the same levels of identity theft and financial fraud——

Senator BROWN. Well, tell me more about Europe. My understanding is European countries, as you have suggested, have stricter data privacy laws; they, I assume, still have functioning credit markets. Right?

Mr. ROTENBERG. Yes, they do.

Senator BROWN. Do these three agencies that Mr. Smith—and Mr. Smith can certainly respond to this, too. These three agencies that he represents, Equifax, TransUnion, and Experian, do they do business in those countries?

Mr. ROTENBERG. I do not know about those specific firms. I do know that there is a vibrant credit market across the European economy. The key is that they are held to a higher standard. For example, in the area of breach notification, Equifax took more than 6 weeks once they learned of the breach to tell American consumers what had happened. Under the new European Union privacy law, they have 72 hours when they confront a problem like that. So you can still operate your business. You are just held to a higher standard.

Senator BROWN. Mr. Smith, the three agencies, let us talk predominantly about those three because they clearly corner the market, more or less. Are they profitable in Europe with a different business model, one with stricter privacy laws?

Mr. SMITH. I do not know whether they—I know that some operate in the U.K. We have a different group of credit reporting agencies in Europe, and it is not necessarily the three that we are familiar with here. We know that Equifax is in the U.K. I am not sure about continental Europe.

Senator BROWN. Could you give to the Committee from those three clients specifically what they do in Europe and their profit—how big a presence they have, market share, like you know in the U.S., and how they are doing in Europe in terms of profitability and any public plans they have about continuing——

Mr. SMITH. Sure, we can do that.

One thing that I would say about Europe, though—and Professor Rotenberg may disagree with this—I do not believe that there is a right to be forgotten with respect to credit report information, that there is a balancing of legitimate interests for collecting such information and a balancing with this right to be forgotten. So there is guidance in the EU that I believe would not permit consumers to just delete wholesale information from credit reporting agencies because of the vital role that they play in managing safety and soundness.

Mr. ROTENBERG. Actually, if I may disagree, that is not correct. The General Data Protection Regulation, the new European Union law, speaks specifically of the right to erasure. Credit reporting agencies are controllers and processors of personal data; they are subject to that. Also under the European law, consumers have the right to an explanation of the basis of a decision. In other words, if a company has an automated process to decide whether someone gets a loan or gets a job, under the European law consumers get to know what the factors were that were used to make that determination.

I think we need to move toward that approach in the United States. I think it would make the companies more accountable. I think it would make the decisions about American consumers fairer and more transparent.

Mr. SMITH. By the way, we do that here, too. We do have requirements that when you take adverse action based on consumer report information, that you notify the consumer. And in the case of where a credit score is used, you have to have the key factors that affected that score.

Senator BROWN. All right. Thank you. And I have one last question. I apologize, and I know I committed to the Chair to keep it as close to 5 minutes as I could. A last question for Mr. Smith. If the FCRA bill that capped liabilities had passed, how much would the 145 million Americans, 5 million in my State, how much would those victims of the Equifax problem been entitled to?

Mr. SMITH. Well, first, you are assuming that there would be a cause of action under the Fair Credit Reporting Act, and right now, based on news reports, there would be no cause of action under the Fair Credit Reporting Act because it was not credit report—the consumer reporting data base that was compromised. Were there to be a breach of a consumer reporting data base, I believe that the figure was—a million? OK. The cap was either $500,000 or $1 million, but it was consistent with all of the other consumer credit protection statutes.

Senator BROWN. OK. Sounds like we have a loophole to close.

Thank you all. Members of the Banking Committee may have questions for you. We encourage them to get them in writing quickly to each of you, within the next 7 days, and please answer as quickly as you can, including some, Mr. Smith, I asked you for.

I thank Chairman Crapo, and the meeting is adjourned.

[Whereupon, at 11:53 a.m., the hearing was adjourned.]

[Prepared statements, responses to written questions, and additional material supplied for the record follow:]

PREPARED STATEMENT OF ANDREW M. SMITH

PARTNER, COVINGTON & BURLING LLP, ON BEHALF OF THE CONSUMER DATA
INDUSTRY ASSOCIATION

OCTOBER 17, 2017

Chairman Crapo, Ranking Member Brown, and Members of the Committee, thank you for the opportunity to appear before you. My name is Andrew Smith, and I am a partner at the law firm Covington & Burling LLP, where I co-chair the Financial Institutions Practice Group. I also serve as the Chair of the Consumer Financial Services Committee of the American Bar Association, and I am a Fellow of the American College of Consumer Financial Services Lawyers. Earlier in my career, I worked at the Federal Trade Commission (FTC), where I was in charge of the FTC's credit reporting program.

I am appearing today on behalf of the Consumer Data Industry Association.

CDIA is an international trade association with over 140 corporate members—including the three nationwide credit bureaus—that educates policymakers, consumers, and others on the benefits of using consumer data responsibly. CDIA members provide businesses with the information and analytical tools necessary to manage risk and protect consumers. CDIA member products are used in more than nine billion transactions each year and expand consumers' access to financial services in a manner that is innovative and focused on their needs. We commend you for holding this hearing, and welcome the opportunity to share our views.

Today, I want to focus on three key points:

- The American credit reporting system provides critically important benefits to consumers and is indispensable to the economy.
- Nationwide credit reporting companies must comply with robust data security standards, because of the direct requirements of Federal and State law, but also because of obligations imposed on credit reporting companies by their customers, such as banks who are required by their prudential regulators to audit the data security of their vendors.
- Beyond these data security requirements, credit reporting companies are subject to a pervasive regulatory and supervisory scheme that effectively protects both consumers and the economy, and has persisted for nearly 50 years.

The National Credit Reporting System

The national credit reporting system is vital to the health of the economy and to maintaining consumer access to credit. More than two-thirds of U.S. gross domestic product comes from consumer spending, a fact that depends in large part on consumer access to affordable credit. In turn, access to credit on reasonable terms makes it affordable for consumers to make important purchases, such as a home or a car, or even a smartphone.

The credit reporting system is so central to the modern American economy that it can be easy to miss its benefits. For example, today we would never imagine that a cross-country move might make it difficult or even impossible to rent an apartment, get utilities connected, or obtain a bank account. But before the development of the modern system, moving to a new city potentially meant losing access to critical services and benefits. Without ready access to a consumer report, lenders, landlords, community banks, credit unions, insurance companies, and others had no assurance that you were conscientious and reliable, unless they knew you personally. As Consumer Financial Protection Bureau (CFPB) Director Richard Cordray has stated,

> Without credit reporting, consumers would not be able to get credit except from those who have already had direct experience with them, for example from local merchants who know whether or not they regularly pay their bills. This was the case fifty or a hundred years ago with "store credit," or when consumers really only had the option of going to their local bank. But now, consumers can instantly access credit because lenders everywhere can look to credit scores to provide a uniform benchmark for assessing risk.[1]

The modern credit reporting system has made it possible for many middle-class consumers to get credit at rates that previously would have been reserved for the wealthy. Now, even those of modest means who have shown themselves to be dili-

---

[1] Richard Cordray, CFPB, Prepared Remarks by Richard Cordray on Credit Reporting (Jul. 16, 2012), *https://www.consumerfinance.gov/about-us/newsroom/prepared-remarks-by-richard-cordray-on-credit-reporting/*.

gent and conscientious with their money can get affordable credit quickly and with a minimum of effort. Furthermore, in recent years, many credit reporting companies have developed tools to provide lenders with information on the unbanked and other consumers without the type of records that typically make up a traditional credit report. These tools allow more consumers to access traditional loans and bank products.

Our credit reporting system today is the envy of the world. It is a key reason why we have such a diverse base of lenders, in contrast to the financial systems of other developed Nations. Our system also provides a disproportionate benefit to smaller financial institutions like community banks and credit unions, who have access to accurate and complete data on par with what very large banks have access to. Our financial system works because companies share critical information across the system to benefit everyone.

Ultimately, credit reports tell the story of our good choices and hard work. They speak for us as consumers when we apply for loans and lenders don't know who we are or if we've paid our bills in the past. Further, credit reports are a check on human bias and assumptions that provide lenders with a foundation of facts that tell our story and contribute to equitable treatment for consumers. CDIA members work to act in the best interests of consumers—by ensuring the accuracy and completeness of data in consumer reports, and by providing businesses with the information that they need to ensure consumers are treated fairly.

Data Security Requirements for Credit Reporting Companies

We understand that the Committee is particularly interested in understanding the data security requirements and standards that apply to credit reporting companies and the steps these companies take to protect consumer data. Under Federal, State, and private contractual frameworks, credit reporting companies are required to protect the sensitive consumer information that they possess, such as by developing, maintaining, and testing the effectiveness of comprehensive information security programs. These existing frameworks combine to form a robust and comprehensive set of cyberstandards that protect the data collected, maintained, and transmitted by credit reporting companies.

The Gramm–Leach–Bliley Act and FTC Safeguards Rule

Credit reporting companies are financial institutions subject to the information security requirements of the Gramm–Leach–Bliley Act (GLBA) and its implementing regulation, the Standards for Safeguarding Customer Information (Safeguards Rule) promulgated by the FTC.[2] The Safeguards Rule imposes specific standards designed to (1) ensure the security and confidentiality of customer records and information; (2) protect against any anticipated threats or hazards to the security or integrity of such records; and (3) protect against unauthorized access to or use of such records or information which could result in substantial harm or inconvenience to any consumer.[3]

The Safeguards Rule requires financial institutions to "develop, implement, and maintain a comprehensive information security program" that includes appropriate administrative, technical, and physical safeguards to achieve these objectives.[4] This program is required to be tailored to the institution's size and complexity, the nature and scope of its activities, and the sensitivity of any customer information at issue.[5]

In addition, a financial institution must designate an employee to coordinate the program; identify reasonably foreseeable risks to the security of the information and assess the sufficiency of safeguards; and design, implement, and regularly test safeguards to protect against such risks.[6] Finally, the Safeguards Rule obligates financial institutions to oversee their service providers' cybersecurity practices, both by taking reasonable steps to ensure the institutions only deal with service providers

---

[2] 15 U.S.C. §6801; 16 CFR pt. 314. The Safeguards Rule applies to financial institutions within the FTC's jurisdiction, which includes credit reporting companies. The Federal prudential banking regulators—i.e., the Federal Reserve, the Office of the Comptroller of the Currency, and the Federal Deposit Insurance Corporation—have promulgated similar information security guidance that applies to the financial institutions under their supervision. See Interagency Guidelines Establishing Information Security Standards, 12 CFR pt. 30, App. B (interagency guidelines as promulgated by the OCC); 12 CFR pt. 208, App. D-2 (as promulgated by the Federal Reserve); 12 CFR pt. 364, App. B (as promulgated by the FDIC).
[3] 15 U.S.C. §6801(b); 16 CFR §314.4(b).
[4] 16 CFR §314.3(a).
[5] See id.
[6] 16 CFR §314.4.

that employ strong security practices, and by entering into contracts with such providers that require them to implement appropriate safeguards. [7]

The FTC Act

Credit reporting companies are also subject to jurisdiction over cybersecurity matters asserted by the FTC under Section 5 of the FTC Act. [8] Pursuant to this statute, the FTC is empowered to take action against any business that engages in "unfair or deceptive acts or practices" (UDAP), which the agency has interpreted to include inadequate data security practices. [9]

The FTC requires that a company employ safeguards for data that are "reasonable in light of the sensitivity and volume of consumer information it holds, the size and complexity of its data operations, and the cost of available tools to improve security and reduce vulnerabilities." [10] While specific cybersecurity requirements under Section 5 are not codified, the FTC has issued detailed guidance that explains what it considers to be reasonable cybersecurity safeguards. These include practices such as encryption, use of firewalls, use of breach detection systems, maintaining physical security of objects that contain sensitive information, and training employees to protect such information. [11] In addition to issuing detailed guidance, the FTC zealously enforces these standards, having brought over 60 cases since 2002 against businesses for putting consumer data at "unreasonable risk." [12]

Fair Credit Reporting Act: Credentialing and Disposal Requirements

The Fair Credit Reporting Act (FCRA) requires that credit reporting companies only provide credit reports to people with a permissible purpose to receive such reports, such as credit or insurance underwriting. More importantly, the law requires that every credit reporting company maintain reasonable procedures designed to ensure that credit reports are provided only to legitimate people for legitimate purposes. These procedures must require that prospective users of credit reports identify themselves, certify the purposes for which the information is sought, and certify that the information will be used for no other purpose. The FTC has brought numerous actions over the years seeking to enforce these provisions, most notably against ChoicePoint, which was alleged to have unwittingly sold credit reports to a ring of identity thieves. In the ChoicePoint case, the FTC collected millions of dollars in consumer redress and civil penalties, including a $10 million civil penalty in connection with the unauthorized disclosure of "nearly 10,000 credit reports," which were allegedly sold by ChoicePoint to persons without a permissible purpose. [13]

The nationwide credit bureaus, and credit reporting companies generally, take these "credentialing" responsibilities very seriously. In addition, the nationwide credit bureaus have been examined by the CFPB with respect to the strength and resiliency of their credentialing procedures. As a part of their credentialing procedures, credit reporting companies maintain detailed written procedures which take into account the risks presented by prospective users and their proposed uses of data. These procedures routinely include:

- site visits to ensure the premises are consistent with the stated business of the prospective customer;
- review of public information sources and public filings to confirm licensure and good standing;
- review of company websites and other public-facing materials;
- checking financial references, including credit reports of owners for certain types of companies, such as those that are not publicly traded;

---

[7] 16 CFR §314.4(d).

[8] 15 U.S.C. §45.

[9] See id.; see also Cong. Res. Serv., "The Federal Trade Commission's Regulation of Data Security Under Its Unfair or Deceptive Acts or Practices (UDAP) Authority" (Sept. 11, 2014), *https://fas.org/sgp/crs/misc/R43723.pdf.*

[10] Fed. Trade Comm'n, Data Security (accessed Dec. 15, 2016), *https://www.ftc.gov/datasecurity.*

[11] See, e.g., Fed. Trade Comm'n, "Protecting Personal Information: A Guide for Business" (Oct. 2016), *https://www.ftc.gov/tips-advice/business-center/guidance/protecting-personal-information-guide-business.*

[12] See Fed. Trade Comm'n, "Privacy and Data Security Update—2016" (Jan. 2017), *https://www.ftc.gov/reports/privacy-data-security-update-2016.*

[13] See Fed. Trade Comm'n., "ChoicePoint Settles Data Security Breach Charges; To Pay $10 Million in Civil Penalties, $5 Million for Consumer Redress" (Jan. 26, 2006), *https://www.ftc.gov/news-events/press-releases/2006/01/choicepoint-settles-data-security-breach-charges-pay-10-million.*

- specific and detailed contractual representations and warranties, as well as specific certifications, that credit report information will be used only for specified purposes;
- detailed customer on-boarding and training procedures; and
- ongoing monitoring of customers—including transaction testing—to ensure that customers are in fact using credit reports for legitimate and permissible purposes.

In addition to these credentialing requirements, the FCRA prohibits credit reporting companies—and anyone else handling credit report information—from disposing of that information in a manner that is not secure.[14] More specifically, the FTC has made a rule providing that a person who maintains or otherwise possesses credit report information, or information derived from credit reports, must properly dispose of such information by taking reasonable measures to protect against the unauthorized access to or use of the information in connection with its disposal.[15]

State Law—State Attorney General Enforcement and Breach Notification

In addition to these Federal regulatory frameworks, credit reporting companies also have numerous data security obligations under State law. First, credit reporting companies may be subject to data security enforcement of State "mini-FTC Acts" that prohibit unfair or deceptive acts or practices.[16] Further, at least 13 States require businesses that own, license, or maintain personal information to implement and maintain reasonable security procedures and practices and to protect personal information from unauthorized access, destruction, use, modification, or disclosure.[17] The majority of States require businesses to dispose of sensitive personal information securely.[18]

Moreover, nearly every U.S. State, the District of Columbia, and several U.S. territories have enacted laws requiring notification to affected individuals following a breach of personal information.[19] These laws typically exempt institutions that are supervised by the Federal prudential regulators. In contrast, credit reporting companies—which are not supervised by the prudential regulators—must comply with the patchwork of more than four dozen breach notification laws if a breach does occur.

Contractual Obligations Imposed Due to Other Regulatory Frameworks

Even beyond these direct legal requirements, the three nationwide credit bureaus—Experian, Equifax, and Transunion—are also subject to substantial additional requirements that result from doing business with other major financial institutions. The information security programs at many credit bureau customers are supervised by Federal prudential regulators, i.e., the Federal Reserve, the Office of the Comptroller of the Currency, the Federal Deposit Insurance Corporation, or the National Credit Union Administration. Under comprehensive and detailed information security standards published by the Federal Financial Institutions Council (FFIEC)—an interagency body of financial regulators—these financial institutions must oversee the information security programs of their third-party service providers.[20] Pursuant to these FFIEC requirements, financial institutions and their auditors subject the nationwide credit bureaus to dozens of information security audits each year, many of which include on-site inspections or examinations, which may take place over a period of several days.

---

[14] See FCRA §628.

[15] See 16 CFR §682.3.

[16] See, e.g., Xavier Becerra, Attorney General, Cal. Dep't of Justice, Target Settles Record $18.5 Million Credit Card Data Breach Case (May 23, 2017), *https://oag.ca.gov/news/press-releases/attorney-general-becerra-target-settles-record-185-million-credit-card-data.*

[17] See Nat'l Conf. of State Legis., Data Security Laws—Private Sector (Jan. 16, 2017), *http://www.ncsl.org/research/telecommunications-and-information-technology/data-security-laws.aspx.*

[18] See Nat'l Conf. of State Legis., Data Disposal Laws (Dec. 1, 2016), *http://www.ncsl.org/research/telecommunications-and-information-technology/data-disposal-laws.aspx.* At the Federal level, the FTC's Disposal Rule regulates the proper disposal of consumer report information. See 16 CFR pt. 682.

[19] See Nat'l Conf. of State Legis., Security Breach Notification Laws (Apr. 12, 2017), *http://www.ncsl.org/research/telecommunications-and-information-technology/security-breach-notification-laws.aspx.*

[20] See FFIEC, IT Examination Handbook Infobase, Information Security: Oversight of Third-Party Service Providers, *https://ithandbook.ffiec.gov/it-booklets/information-security/ii-information-security-program-management/iic-risk-mitigation/iic20-oversight-of-third-party-service-providers.aspx.*

The Payment Card Industry Data Security Standard

The three nationwide credit bureaus also comply with the Payment Card Industry Data Security Standard (PCI DSS). The PCI DSS is a set of cybersecurity requirements that are mandatory for all organizations that store, process, and transmit sensitive payment card information of the major credit card associations. [21] The standard requires credit reporting companies to take a number of specific steps to ensure the security of certain data. For example, the PCI DSS requires members to install and maintain firewalls, encrypt the transmission of cardholder data, protect against malware and implement and update anti-virus programs, restrict both digital and physical access to cardholder data, regularly test security systems and processes, and maintain a detailed information security policy for all personnel. [22] The standard imposes further detailed and specific technical requirements for the protection of cardholder data, such as a restriction on service providers' storage of personal identification or card verification numbers after card authorization. [23] In addition, the standard requires a service provider to ensure that any third parties with whom it shares data also comply with the PCI DSS. [24]

All three of the nationwide credit bureaus have been certified by the card networks as "PCI DSS Validated Service Providers," meaning that they are approved to store, process and transmit cardholder data. Service providers that store, process, or transmit cardholder data must be registered with the card networks and demonstrate PCI DSS compliance. PCI DSS compliance validation is required every 12 months for all service providers. As an example, all three nationwide credit bureaus are included on the Visa Service Provider Registry, indicating that they have successfully validated PCI DSS compliance with an on-site assessment, based on the report of an independent Qualified Security Assessor (QSA), and have met all applicable Visa program requirements. [25]

The Fair Credit Reporting Act and CFPB Supervision

Finally, I want to discuss the consumer protection regime that applies to credit reporting companies under the FCRA. This regime has persisted for nearly 50 years, with occasional fine tuning and two significant revisions, in 1996 and 2003. In addition, in 2012, the CFPB began supervising the credit reporting companies for, among other things, compliance with the FCRA.

When the credit reporting industry first began in the United States, there was little standardization in the methods used and types of data collected. In particular, there was no standard procedure for consumers to find out what was in their credit report and to have erroneous information corrected. In response to these concerns, in 1970 Congress passed the FCRA, which imposed duties on credit reporting companies (referred to as "consumer reporting agencies" under the statute). [26] These duties included providing consumers transparency by requiring lenders and other users of credit reports to notify consumers when they take "adverse action" based on a credit report, providing consumers with access to their file, and providing for a mechanism for consumers to dispute and correct inaccurate or incomplete information.

Building on the core structure of the FCRA, Congress revised the statute in 1996. One of the most important revisions was to impose a set of duties, not just on the credit reporting companies themselves, but on those businesses that furnished the information to the credit bureaus in the first place. [27] In 2003, again building on the FCRA's core structure, Congress again modified the FCRA through the Fair and Accurate Credit Transactions Act, which added certain consumer protections such as free annual credit reports and new protections for identity theft victims. [28]

Under the FCRA, credit reporting companies are subject to a comprehensive regulatory regime that provides many protections to consumers. A number of these provisions are designed to protect consumer privacy, such as the aforementioned per-

---

[21] Payment Card Industry Security Standards Council, "Requirements and Security Assessment Procedures", Version 3.2 (Apr. 2016).

[22] Id. at 5.

[23] See, e.g., id. at 38–39.

[24] Id. at 12.

[25] See, e.g., Visa Global Registry of Service Providers, *https://www.visa.com/splisting/index.html.*

[26] See "Fair Credit Reporting Act: How It Functions for Consumers and the Economy", Hearing Before the Subcomm. on Financial Institutions and Consumer Credit of the H. Comm. on Financial Services, 108th Cong. 129 (2003) (prepared statement of the Federal Trade Commission).

[27] See, e.g., "Amending Fair Credit Reporting Act", Sen. Comm. on Banking, Housing, and Urban Aff's, S. Rept. 108–166 (Oct. 17, 2003).

[28] See FCRA §609(e).

missible purpose and credentialing requirements. The FCRA also includes criminal penalties for people who obtain credit reports under false pretenses or credit reporting companies that knowingly provide credit reports to persons not authorized to receive them, for example, by selling consumers' private information to a litigation opponent or an ex-spouse hoping to find embarrassing information. To further ensure consumer privacy is protected, as I discussed before, credit reporting companies must "credential" users of their consumer reports to confirm they in fact have a permissible purpose to obtain the reports. [29]

Many of the provisions also address the accuracy and completeness of consumer reports. The most basic of these protections is the consumer's right to know what is in his or her file. [30] The 2003 amendments to the FCRA additionally required nationwide credit bureaus and nationwide specialty credit bureaus to provide consumers with free annual disclosures of the information in their file, including through an official website, *www.annualcreditreport.com*. Further, when a user of a consumer report takes "adverse action" against a consumer on the basis of information in his or her credit report, that user must provide the consumer with a notice that contains information about how the consumer can obtain a copy of his or her credit report and can get errors corrected. [31] For example, if a lender denies a consumer's application because of a low credit score, the lender must provide the consumer with a notice of adverse action. In addition, consumers have the right to dispute the contents of their file, and the credit reporting company is obligated to conduct a reasonable investigation of the dispute. [32] Credit reporting companies must also independently employ reasonable procedures to maintain the maximum possible accuracy of the information in consumer files. [33]

Finally, in 2012, the CFPB became the first supervisor of the national credit reporting system—the first regulator with examination authority over the credit reporting companies, the users of credit reports, and the companies that furnish information into the credit reporting companies for incorporation into credit reports. [34] Since the CFPB formalized its supervisory authority in January 2012, the nationwide credit bureaus have been subject to essentially continuous examination cycles, where they have been examined for the adequacy of their compliance management systems, their dispute handling procedures, their procedures to ensure the maximum possible accuracy of credit reports, their credentialing procedures, and other important and highly regulated functions. In this supervisory role, the CFPB examines the policies, procedures, controls, and practices of credit reporting companies. The companies expend substantial resources responding to examiner requests and must maintain transparency with their examiners. If the examiners discover any areas in which a credit reporting company is not living up to its obligations, the CFPB can resolve the issue through the supervisory process, or, if the issue is sufficiently serious, choose to bring a public enforcement action. The Bureau recently opined on the success of this regime, concluding that it had produced a "proactive approach to compliance management" that "will reap benefits for consumers—and the lenders that use consumer reports—for many years to come." [35]

Thank you again for the opportunity to testify before you today. I am happy to answer any questions.

———

PREPARED STATEMENT OF MARC ROTENBERG

PRESIDENT, ELECTRONIC PRIVACY INFORMATION CENTER

OCTOBER 17, 2017

Mister Chairman and Members of the Committee, thank you for the opportunity to testify today concerning consumer data security and the credit bureaus. My name is Marc Rotenberg. I am President of the Electronic Privacy Information Center (EPIC). EPIC is an independent nonprofit research organization in Washington, DC, established in 1994 to focus public attention on emerging privacy and civil liberties issues. I have also taught information privacy law at Georgetown University Law

---

[29] See FCRA §607(a).
[30] See FCRA §609.
[31] See FCRA §615(a).
[32] See FCRA §611.
[33] See FCRA §607(b).
[34] The CFPB has supervisory authority over "larger participants" in the consumer reporting industry, which are defined in 12 CFR §1090.104.
[35] See CFPB, Supervisory Highlights: Consumer Reporting Special Edition, Winter 2017 3 (Mar. 2017), *http://files.consumerfinance.gov/f/documents/201703\cfpb\Supervisory-Highlights-Consumer-Reporting-Special-Edition.pdf.*

Center since 1990 and I am the author of several leading books on privacy law.[1] I testified before this Committee in 2011 following the spate of data breaches in the financial services sector.[2] And in a recent article for the Harvard Business Review, I outlined several steps that Congress could take in response to the Equifax data breach.[3]

I will say at the outset that the Equifax data breach is one of the most serious in the Nation's history, on par with the breach at the Office of Personnel Management in 2015 that impacted 22.5 million Federal employees, their friends and family members. The Equifax breach poses enormous challenges to the security of American families, as well as our countries national security. Privacy, more precisely described as "data protection," is no longer simply about the concern that large companies misuse personal data. Today our country is facing cyberattacks from foreign adversaries and it is the personal data stored by companies that is the target. When these companies engage in lax security practices or freely disclose consumer data without consent, they are placing not only consumers, but also our Nation at risk.

There is no simple solution to these challenges, but in my testimony today I will outline the steps that I believe Congress could take to minimize the risk flowing from this breach and address the risk of future breaches in the data broker industry. In brief, current laws do not protect consumers. Legislation should (1) give consumers greater control of their personal data held by others; (2) limit the use of the Social Security Number in the private sector; (3) minimize the collection of personally identifiable information; (4) improve breach notification; and (5) change the defaults in the credit reporting industry with (a) default credit "freezes" that give consumers opt-in control over the release of their credit report, (b) free, routine monitoring services, and (c) free access at any time for any purpose to a consumer who wants to see the complete contents of a credit report or other similar information product made available for sale.

I. The Implications of the Equifax Breach

A. *This Breach Was Unprecedented in Scope*

The Equifax data breach is one of the most significant in the history of the United States. Over 145 million American consumers were impacted.[4] More than four months passed from the time the Equifax failed to install critical software updates till the time the time the problem was addressed. And the data that was disclosed is precisely the information that individuals rely upon to open bank accounts, get car loans, seek employment, buy cell phones, and even issue checks online. The data included:

- Names
- Social Security Numbers
- Birth Dates
- Addresses, and
- Driver's License Numbers.[5]

This data is a gold mine for identity thieves. The widespread availability of this personal data poses an ongoing risk to American families and creates problems for those who suffer identity theft that will take months, if not years, to resolve.

The Equifax breach also has implications for U.S. trade relations. According to the Canadian Broadcast Corporation, the data of 100,000 Canadians was seized in the breach.[6] The British Broadcasting Corporation reported that 400,000 U.K. con-

---

[1] Anita Allen and Marc Rotenberg, "Privacy Law an Society" (West 2016); Marc Rotenberg, "The Privacy Law Sourcebook: United States Law", *International Law, and Recent Developments* (Epic 2016); Marc Rotenberg, Et al., "Privacy and the Modern Age: The Search for Solutions" (The New Press 2015).

[2] "Cybersecurity and Data Protection in the Financial Services Sector", Hearing Before the S. Comm. on Banking, Housing, and Urban Affairs, 112th Cong. (2011) (statement of Marc Rotenberg, Exec. Dir., EPIC), *https://epic.org/privacy/testimony/ EPIC_Senate_Banking_Testimony%20 6 21 11.pdf.*

[3] Marc Rotenberg, "Equifax, the Credit Reporting Industry, and What Congress Should Do Next", *Harv. Bus. Rev.* (Sept. 20, 2017), *https://hbr.org/2017/09/equifax-the-credit-reporting-industry-and-what-congress-should-do-next.*

[4] Equifax, "Equifax Announces Cybersecurity Incident Involving Consumer Information" (Sept. 7, 2017), *https://investor.equifax.com/tools/viewpdf.aspx.*

[5] Id.

[6] Matthew Braga, "100,000 Canadian Victims: What We Know About the Equifax Breach—And What We Don't", CBC News (Sept. 19, 2017), *http://www.cbc.ca/news/technology/equifax-canada-breach-sin-cybersecurity-what-we-know-1.4297532.*

sumers were affected by the Equifax breach. [7] Equifax has since stated that 15,200,000 million U.K. consumers were impacted by the breach. [8] And all of this at a time when foreign Government are carefully scrutinizing U.S. data protection to determine to determine whether it is safe to transfer personal data to the United States. Equifax has given other countries good reason to fear their data being entrusted to U.S. companies. That could harm U.S. trade.

B. Equifax Was at Fault

Equifax is clearly responsible this breach. The company was notified of the vulnerability in its software but failed to make the required fixes. Hackers accessed the Equifax database by exploiting a known security vulnerability. [9] The Apache Software Foundation issued a statement in March announcing the vulnerability, and the patch was made available the same day. [10] The Department of Homeland Security also contacted the three credit reporting agencies back in March to notify them of the vulnerability. Yet Equifax left the vulnerability unpatched until July 29. By that time the attackers had already seized millions of records over several months.

It is also worth emphasizing that Equifax chose to collect this data on American customers—American consumers did not choose to provide their personal data to Equifax. Also, Equifax pursued a security strategy that allowed a single point of failure to permit the breach of more than half of the Nation's credit reports.

Equifax's response to the breach also demonstrated the company's incompetence and indifference to data security. Equifax created a separate domain— "equifaxsecurity2017.com"—where consumers were required to enter their name and the last six digits of their social security number to find out if their information was compromised. The domain was not registered to Equifax and was running on WordPress, causing many browsers to flag it as a phishing threat.

To demonstrate how easily this domain could be spoofed, a developer bought the domain "securityequifax2017.com" and made it look exactly like the real Equifax support page. [11] The Equifax even tweeted a link of the fraudulent website, thinking it was their own.

Security researchers later discovered that Equifax's website has also been hacked, and contained false Adobe Flash download links that trick users into downloading malware that displays unwanted ads online. [12] Furthermore, consumers who contacted Equifax to freeze their credit were given PINs to use when they wanted to unfreeze their credit. These pins were based on the time and date of the freeze, making them easier to guess. [13] These actions after the breach reveal how poorly prepared the company was to assist consumers. The company's efforts to mitigate damage caused by the breach have exposed millions of Americans to even more risk.

C. Equifax Breach Increases the Likelihood of Identity Theft in the United States

The Equifax breach will cause unprecedented harm to consumers. When hackers get access to credit card numbers they can rack up fraudulent charges, but consumers are able to cancel their credit cards and get new numbers. By contrast, consumers cannot change their social security numbers or dates of birth. Equifax's victims are exposed to ongoing identity theft and fraud, and the full effects of the damage will not be known for years.

---

[7] "Equifax Says Almost 400,000 Britons Hit in Data Breach", BBC News (Sept. 15, 2017), *http://www.bbc.com/news/technology-41286638.*

[8] Equifax, Equifax Ltd (U.K.): "Update Regarding the Ongoing Investigation Into Us Cybersecurity Incident" (Oct. 10, 2017), *https://www.equifax.co.uk/about-equifax/press-releases/en\gb/-/blogs/equifax-ltd-uk-update-regarding-the-ongoing-investigation-into-us-cyber-security-incident.*

[9] The Apache Software Foundation Blog, "MEDIA ALERT: The Apache Software Foundation Confirms Equifax Data Breach Due to Failure to Install Patches Provided for Apache Struts™ Exploit" (Sept. 14, 2017), *https://blogs.apache.org/foundation/entry/media-alert-the-apache- software.*

[10] Id.

[11] Alfred NG, "Equifax Sends Breach Victims to Fake Support Site", CNET (Sept. 20, 2017), *https://www.cnet.com/news/equifax-twitter-fake-support-site-breach-victims/.*

[12] Dan Goodin, "Equifax Website Borked Again, This Time To Redirect to Fake Flash Update", ArsTechnica (Oct. 12, 2017), *https://arstechnica.com/information-technology/2017/10/equifax-website-hacked-again-this-time-to-redirect-to-fake-flash-update/.*

[13] Ron Lieber, "After Equifax, Here's Your Next Worry: Weak PINs", *N.Y. Times* (Sept. 10, 2017), *https://www.nytimes.com/2017/09/10/your-money/identity-theft/equifax-breach-credit-freeze.html?rref=collection%2Fbyline%2Fron-lieber.*

Identity theft is an enormous problem for consumers. The Federal Trade Commission reported 399,225 cases of identity theft in the United States in 2016. [14] Of that number, 29 percent involved the use of personal data to commit tax fraud. More than 32 percent reported that their data was used to commit credit card fraud, up sharply from 16 percent in 2015. A 2015 report from the Department of Justice found that 86 percent of the victims of identity theft experienced the fraudulent use of existing account information, such as credit card or bank account information. [15] The same report estimated the cost to the U.S. economy at $15.4 billion.

Identity theft can completely derail a person's financial future. Criminals who have gained access to others' personally identifiable information can open bank accounts and credit cards, take out loans, and conduct other financial activities using someone else's identity. Identity theft has severe consequences for consumers, including: [16]

- Being denied of credit cards and loans
- Being unable to rent an apartment or find housing
- Paying increased interest rates on existing credit cards
- Having greater difficulty getting a job
- Suffering severe distress and anxiety

II. The Equifax Breach Underscores the Need for Reform

The credit reporting industry is in urgent need of reform. An industry that collects the most sensitive data of Americans and has such a great impact on the U.S. economy must use state of the art security measures and must give consumer control over the personal data. Instead, credit bureaus cut corners on security, capture the upside value of selling credit reports, and transfer the risk to consumers for breaches and errors. As companies increasingly rely on complex consumer profiling techniques, credit bureaus have amassed vast amounts of personal data. Without comprehensive legislation, the data breach problem will only get worse.

A. Data Breaches Are an Epidemic in the United States

The scope of the data breach problem extends well beyond Equifax. Data breaches are occurring more frequently across a number of industries. According to the Identity Theft Resource Center, data breaches in the United States increased by 40 percent in 2016 to a record high of 1,093. [17] As companies collect more data, the risk of identity theft is almost certain to increase.

- The 2013 Yahoo breach, in which hackers stole names, birth dates, phone numbers, and passwords, is now estimated to have impacted all 3 billion users, making it the largest data breach on record. [18]

- In 2015, a data breach at the Office of Personnel Management compromised the personal data, including biometric identifiers, of more than 20 million people, many of them with security clearances. [19]

- Recent data breaches have affected Chipotle, Home Depot, and Target, impacting over 100 million stolen credit card numbers combined. [20]

---

[14] Fed. Trade Comm'n, "FTC Releases Annual Summary of Consumer Complaints" (March 3, 2017), *https://www.ftc.gov/news-events/press-releases/2017/03/ftc-releases-annual-summary-consumer-complaints.*

[15] Erika Harrell, "Bureau of Justice Statistics, Victims of Identity Theft", 2014 (Sept. 27, 2015), *https://www.bjs.gov/index.cfm?ty=pbdetail&iid=5408.*

[16] Identity Theft Resource Center, "Identity Theft: The Aftermath 2017", *http://www.idtheftcenter.org/images/page-docs/Aftermath2017Finalv1.pdf.*

[17] Identity Theft Resource Center, "Data Breaches Increase 40 Percent in 2016, Finds New Report" (Jan. 19, 2017), *http://www.idtheftcenter.org/2016databreaches.html.*

[18] Nicole Pelroth, "All 3 Billion Yahoo Accounts Were Affected by 2013 Attack", *New York Times* (Oct. 3, 2017), *https://www.nytimes.com/2017/10/03/technology/yahoo-hack-3-billion-users.html.*

[19] Ellen Nakashima, "Hacks of OPM Databases Compromised 22.1 Million People, Federal Authorities Say", *Wash. Post* (Jul. 9, 2015), *https://www.washingtonpost.com/news/federal-eye/wp/2015/07/09/hack-of-security-clearance-system-affected-21-5-million-people-federal-authorities-say/.*

[20] Lisa Baertlein, "Chipotle Says Hackers Hit Most Restaurants In Data Breach", Reuters (May 26, 2017), *https://www.reuters.com/article/us-chipotle-cyber/chipotle-says-hackers-hit-most-restaurants-in-data-breach-idUSKBN18M2BY*; Robin Sidel, "Home Depot's 56 Million Card Breach Bigger Than Target's", *Wall Street J.* (Sep. 18, 2014), *https://www.wsj.com/articles/home-depot-breach-bigger-than-targets-1411073571*; "Target: 40 Million Credit Cards Compromised", CNN (Dec. 19, 2013), *http://money.cnn.com/2013/12/18/news/companies/target-credit-card/index.html.*

- Data breaches have also impacted large banks, educational institutions, health care providers, and many other businesses. [21]

Data breaches in the credit reporting industry pose an enormous threat to consumers. Credit reporting agencies maintain an extraordinary amount of personal data, including Social Security numbers, birthdates, home addresses, telephone numbers, and driver's license records—information that is the holy grail for identity thieves.

B. Consumers Lack Control Over Their Credit Reports

Despite these risks, consumers cannot protect themselves. The relationship between the credit reporting industry and the consumer is skewed. The industry was built to serve the companies that collect and use consumer information and not the consumers themselves. Businesses have easy access to credit reports while consumers do not. By law, consumers are entitled to only one free credit report per year, and the process of obtaining one is cumbersome. [22] Consumers have no control over what information credit reporting agencies collect. Information is often out of date, incomplete, or inaccurate, and it is often impossible for consumers to correct inaccurate information. [23] Consumers are then wrongfully denied jobs, housing, and credit as a result. In these circumstances, consumers are almost always left in the dark about how their data was used.

Under current law and industry practices, when data breaches occur, consumers bear the burden. Consumers only learn of the breach once the company decides to notify the public, and then must take costly steps to obtain a credit freeze or credit monitoring services. [24] And because consumers cannot choose which companies collect their data, they have no control over how vulnerable their information is to identity thieves. In sum, the current model is broken, and only Congress can fix it. [25]

C. Consumer Profiling Is Growing More Complex and Lacks Transparency

An invisible system of consumer profiling has emerged. [26] We now face the specter of a "scored society" where consumers do not have access to the most basic information about how they are evaluated. [27] Data brokers now use secret algorithms to build profiles on every American citizen whether they have allowed their personal data to be collected or not. [28] These secret algorithms can be used to determine the interest rates on mortgages and credit cards, raise consumers' insurance rates, or even deny people jobs. [29] Data brokers even scrape social media and score consumers based on factors such as their political activity on Twitter. [30]

In one recent complaint to the Federal Trade Commission, EPIC highlighted the practice of the secret scoring of young athletes. [31] It may seem to odd to think that an activity such as high school athletics is now being taken over by proprietary algorithms, but that is in fact the case. Once you could say that a runner completed a mile in 4:28, a high school basketball player shot 92 percent from the line, or a softball player hit .352 for the season. Now it is the secret scoring of young athletes that could determine their future.

---

[21] Greg Farrell and Patricia Hurtado, "JPMorgan's 2014 Hack Tied to Largest Cyber Breach Ever", Bloomberg (Nov. 10, 2015), *https://www.bloomberg.com/news/articles/2015-11-10/hackers-accused-by-u-s-of-targeting-top-banks-mutual-funds*; Brendan Pierson, "Anthem To Pay Record $115 Million To Settle U.S. Lawsuits Over Data Breach", Reuters (June 23, 2017), *https://www.reuters.com/article/us-anthem-cyber-settlement/anthem-to-pay-record-115-million-to-settle-u-s-lawsuits-over-data-breach-idUSKBN19E2ML*; UMD Data Breach, University of Maryland, *http://www.umd.edu.datasecurity/*.

[22] Fed. Trade Comm'n., Free Credit Reports, March 2013, *https://www.consumer.ftc.gov/articles/0155-free-credit-reports*.

[23] Id.

[24] Fed. Trade Comm'n, Credit Freeze FAQs (2017), *https://www.consumer.ftc.gov/articles/0497-credit-freeze-faqs*.

[25] Bruce Schneier, "Don't Waste Your Breath Complaining to Equifax About Data Breach", CNN, Sep. 11, 2017, *http://www.cnn.com/2017/09/11/opinions/dont-complain-to-equifax-demand-government-act-opinion-schneier/index.html*.

[26] Id.

[27] Danielle Keats Citron and Frank Pasquale, "The Scored Society: Due Process for Automated Predictions", 89 *Wash. L. Rev.* 1 (2014).

[28] Id.

[29] "Exploring the Fintech Landscape", Hearing Before the S. Comm. on Banking, Housing, and Urban Affairs, 115th Cong. 7 (2017) (written testimony of Frank Pasquale, Professor of Law, University of Maryland).

[30] Id.

[31] EPIC, "EPIC Asks FTC To Stop System for Secret Scoring of Young Athletes" (May 17, 2017), *https://epic.org/2017/05/epic-asks-ftc-to-stop-system-f.html*.

Determinations about whether we get a job, a home, or an athletic scholarship should not be left to the "secret judgments of software," especially when this type of machine learning can lead to discrimination. [32] We not only lack knowledge of the methods being used to score us, but we do not even know what underlying information about us is being collected. For example, EPIC just filed an amicus brief in a case involving a company that scrapes data from user profiles on LinkedIn to create scores to evaluate "flight risk." [33] The consumer scoring industry—not just the credit reporting agencies—needs oversight, accountability, and transparency. [34]

III. Next Steps To Protect Consumers Following the Equifax Breach

In the wake of the Equifax breach, immediate action should be taken to reform not only the credit reporting industry, but also to address the broader problem of secret profiling and mishandling of consumers' personal data. It is time to change the defaults and time to put consumers back in control of both their credit reports and their personal information. Consumers must have free and easy access to their credit information, and control over when and how that information is disclosed. Companies collecting consumers' personal data must establish effective safeguards, including requirements for prompt disclosure of any data breach. Congress should end the use of the social security number as a general-purpose identifier. And Congress should promote the use of innovative technology to minimize the collection of personal data.

A. Reform the Industry by Giving Consumers Control Over Their Credit Reports

The essential problem with the credit reporting industry is that it does not work. Consumers have no control over the collection and use of their credit reports and bear all the risk when credit reporting agencies mishandle their personal information. Data brokers operate in the shadows and consumers are left in the dark. That structure is backward. Consumers should have free access to their credit information and, by default, no credit report should be released to a third party without the consumer's express authorization.

There are already several commonsense proposals that the Congress should enact into law:

Free Credit "Freezes" and "Thaws" (Change the Default for Report Disclosure to "Opt-in")

Credit reporting agencies should change the default on access to credit reports by third parties. Instead of the current setting, which allows virtually anyone to pull someone's credit report, credit reporting agencies should establish a credit freeze for all disclosures, with free and easy access for consumers who wish to disclose their report for a specific purpose. A credit freeze is one of the only mechanisms available to prevent "new account identity theft" before it happens. [35] But only four States (Indiana, Maine, North Carolina, and South Carolina) mandate free consumer access to credit freezes and thaws, while four additional States "provide free freezes but charge for thaws." [36] This means that "[a]pproximately 158 million consumers between 18–65 in 42 States and D.C. must pay a fee to get credit freezes." [37]

Provide Free Monitoring and Easy Access to Credit History

Current laws allow consumers access to free credit reports, but the process is cumbersome, and few consumers take advantage. A rationalized market would help ensure that consumers have as much information as possible about the use of their personal data by others. Instead, Equifax and other credit reporting agencies profit from the very problems they create. The Consumer Financial Protection Bureau also fined Equifax and TransUnion earlier this year after finding that the companies "lured consumers into costly recurring payments for credit-related products with false promises." [38] Credit reporting agencies should provide life-long credit moni-

---

[32] Frank Pasquale, *The Black Box Society* 8 (2015); Citron and Pasquale, supra.

[33] EPIC, hiQ Labs, Inc. v. LinkedIn Corp., *https://epic.org/amicus/cfaa/linkedin/*.

[34] Citron and Pasquale, supra, at 5.

[35] See U.S. PIRG, "Security Freeze and Identity Theft Tips", *http://uspirg.org/sites/pirg/files/resources/Security%20Freeze%20and%20Identity%20Theft%20Tips.pdf*.

[36] U.S. PIRG, "Interactive Map Shows Consumers in 42 States Have No Access to Free Credit Freezes" (Oct. 2, 2017), *https://uspirg.org/news/usp/interactive-map-shows-consumers-42-states-have-no-access-free-credit-freezes*.

[37] Id.

[38] Consumer Fin. Prot. Bureau, "CFPB Orders TransUnion and Equifax to Pay for Deceiving Consumers in Marketing Credit Scores and Credit Products" (Jan. 3, 2017), *https://www.consumerfinance.gov/about-us/newsroom/cfpb-orders-transunion-and-equifax-pay-deceiving-consumers-marketing-credit-scores-and-credit-products/*.

toring services to consumers at no cost. Some credit card companies already offer similar services for free.[39] The credit other reporting agencies should do so as well.

Mandatory Disclosure of Secret Scores and Algorithms

Congress should move quickly to address the risks to consumers in the credit reporting industry. But the problems in the credit reporting industry arise in other industries. We face the specter of a "scored society" where consumers don't have access to the most basic information about how they are evaluated.[40] "Algorithmic transparency" is key to accountability.[41] Absent rules requiring the disclosure of these secret scores, lists, and the underlying data and algorithms upon which they are based, consumers will have no way to even know, let alone solve, these problems.

B. Improve Breach Notification

The epidemic of data breaches, and failure of companies to be held accountable, cannot continue. Identity theft has reached an unprecedented level, yet the companies that amass troves of personal data expect consumers to bear the costs of breaches. After a data breach occurs, companies such as Equifax urge consumers to check a website to find out whether they were affected.[42] But even these vague warnings come weeks or months after the breach has occurred.[43] That is not a workable business response or sensible public policy.

It has become clear that these companies cannot effectively police themselves. Congress should set national, baseline standards to limit the damage caused by data breaches.

Federal Baseline Data Breach Notification Standard

At a bare minimum, the Equifax breach underscores the need for a baseline Federal data breach notification standard for all companies that store personal information.[44] The only Federal law with a breach notification rule is the Health Insurance Portability and Accountability Act, which only applies to protected health information.[45] Florida currently has one of the most comprehensive data breach laws, providing a mandatory 30-day notification rule, a broad scope, and proactive requirements for reasonable data protection measures.[46] A Federal baseline notification standard should go even further, requiring immediate and efficient notification of impacted consumers, regulators, and the public.[47] Companies are increasingly interacting with consumers on social media and via automated text and email messages, so it is reasonable to expect that companies can notify consumers within 48–72 hours of a breach.

Reasonable Data Security Measures

---

[39] See, e.g., Discover, Social Security Alerts (2017), *https://www.discover.com/credit-cards/member-benefits/security/ssn-newaccount-alerts/*.

[40] Id.

[41] EPIC, "Algorithmic Transparency", *https://epic.org/algorithmic-transparency/*.

[42] These post-breach websites can also create new risks to consumers. See, e.g., Merrit Kennedy, "After Massive Data Breach, Equifax Directed Customers to Fake Site", NPR (Sept. 21, 2017), *http://www.npr.org/sections/thetwo-way/2017/09/21/552681357/after-massive-data-breach-equifax-directed-customers-to-fake-site*.

[43] See, e.g., Michael Hiltzik, "Here Are All The Ways The Equifax Data Breach Is Worse Than You Can Imagine", *L.A. Times* (Sept. 8, 2017), *http://www.latimes.com/business/hiltzik/la-fi-hiltzik-equifax-breach-20170908-story.html*.

[44] There are currently breach notification laws in "[f]orty-eight States, the District of Columbia, Guam, Puerto Rico and the Virgin Islands." Nat'l Conference of State Legislators, Security Breach Notification Laws (Apr. 12, 2017), *http://www.ncsl.org/research/telecommunications-and-information-technology/security-breach-notification-laws.aspx#1*. See also Steptoe and Johnson LLP, "Comparison of U.S. State and Federal Security Breach Notification Laws" (Sept. 1, 2017), *https://www.steptoe.com/assets/htmldocuments/SteptoeDataBreachNotificationChart2017.pdf*.

[45] 45 CFR §§164.400–414. See Steptoe, supra at 202–08. The Gramm–Leach–Bliley Act "Interagency Guidelines" also discuss consumer notice, but the rules do not contain a requirement that notice be given within a specific time period. See 12 CFR pt. 224, app. F (Supp. A 2014); 70 *FR* 15,736 (2005).

[46] EPIC, State Data Breach Notification Policy (2017), *https://epic.org/state-policy/data-breach/*.

[47] "Discussion Draft of H.R.——, A Bill to Require Greater Protection for Sensitive Consumer Data and Timely Notification in Case of Breach", Hearing before the Subcomm. on Commerce, Manufacturing, and Trade of the H. Comm. on Energy and Commerce, 112th Cong. (testimony and statement for the record of Marc Rotenberg, Exec. Dir., EPIC) *https://epic.org/privacy/testimony/EPIC\Testimony\House\Commerce\6-11\Final.pdf; see also "H.R. 2221, the Data Accountability and Trust Act and H.R. 1319, the Informed P2P User Act", Hearing before the Subcomm. on Commerce, Trade, and Consumer Prot. of the H. Comm. on Energy and Commerce, 111th Cong. (2009) (testimony and statement for the record of Marc Rotenberg, Exec. Dir., EPIC), https://epic.org/linkedfiles/rotenberg\house\ctcp2221\1319.pdf*.

Prompt breach notifications are necessary to ensure that consumers and regulators can quickly deal with a data breach after it happens. But more needs to be done to prevent these breaches from happening in the first place. For example, the Florida Information Protection Act requires that companies collecting consumer data "take reasonable measures to protect and secure data in electronic form containing personal information." [48] Companies that collect and store sensitive consumer data are in the best position to prevent data breaches, and they should be held liable when they fail to adopt reasonable security measures. [49] This is especially important because the Equifax hack and other major data breaches caused by known vulnerabilities are entirely preventable. [50]

Elimination of Consumer Arbitration Waivers

The most effective way to improve data security is to establish a private right of action for consumers who have suffered a breach of their personal data. This provides a specific remedy for a specific harm. But Equifax did the exact opposite. In response to the data breach, the company tried to trick consumer into an arbitration agreement, guaranteeing that there would be few legal remedies for consumers following the breach. [51] The Consumer Financial Protection Bureau (CFPB) recently banned arbitration clauses in consumer financial contracts because class action waivers make it prohibitive for any consumers to obtain relief. [52] Credit reporting agencies and other financial institutions should be prohibited from using these arbitration agreements to block consumer actions for breach, improper disclosure, or misuse of their personal data. And a breach of personal data should be sufficient harm to provide a cause of action.

Expansion of Gramm–Leach–Bliley Security Rules

The existing data security requirements for consumer-facing financial institutions should extend to credit reporting agencies and other companies that sell consumer profiles. The Gramm–Leach–Bliley Act already provides for oversight of financial institutions' privacy practices by seven regulatory agencies, but the current regime fails to address credit reporting agencies. [53] Specifically, although the Dodd-Frank Act transferred authority over certain privacy provisions to the CFBP, the law did not transfer regulatory authority to establish data security guidelines. [54] As it stands, the CFPB can only bring enforcement actions based on a company's affirmative misrepresentations about data security practices. [55] Given that credit reporting agencies hold more sensitive personal data than many of the other financial institutions combined, it makes little sense for those companies to be exempt from the rules.

C. Limit the Use of the Social Security Number by Private Companies

Social security numbers have been asked to do too much. They were never meant to be used as an all-purpose identifier. [56] The unregulated use of the social security number in the private sector has contributed to record levels of identity theft and financial fraud. [57] The recent Equifax breach illustrates this problem, as the social

---

[48] Fla. Stat. §501.171(2) (2017). See EPIC, "State Data Breach Notification Policy" (2017).

[49] Brief of Amicus Curiae EPIC in Support of Appellants, Storm v. Paytime, No. 15-3690, at 25–30 (3d Cir. filed Apr. 18, 2016), *https://epic.org/amicus/data-breach/storm/EPIC-Amicus-Storm-Paytime.pdf*.

[50] See Lily Hay Newman, "Equifax Officially Has No Excuse", *Wired* (Sept. 14, 2017), *https://www.wired.com/story/equifax-breach-no-excuse/*.

[51] Equifax is the most recent, but not the only, company guilty of forcing consumers into arbitration against their interests. See David Lazarus, "The Real Outrage Isn't Equifax's Arbitration Clause—It's All The Others", *L.A. Times* (Sept. 12, 2017), *http://www.latimes.com/business/lazarus/la-fi-lazarus-equifax-arbitration-clauses-20170912-story.html*.

[52] 12 CFR 1040; Consumer Fin. Prot. Bureau, "CFPB Study Finds That Arbitration Agreements Limit Relief For Consumers" (Mar. 10, 2015) *https://www.consumerfinance.gov/about-us/newsroom/cfpb-study-finds-that-arbitration-agreements-limit-relief-for-consumers/*.

[53] 15 U.S.C. §6801; see 79 *FR* 37166 (2014) ("Section 501(b) of the Gramm–Leach–Bliley Act (GLB Act) [1] requires the Office of the Comptroller of the Currency, Board of Governors of the Federal Reserve System, Federal Deposit Insurance Corporation, and Office of Thrift Supervision (the Agencies), as well as the National Credit Union, the Securities and Exchange Commission, and the Federal Trade Commission, to establish appropriate standards for the financial institutions subject to their respective jurisdictions relating to the administrative, technical, and physical safeguards for customer records and information.").

[54] Id.

[55] See, e.g., Consumer Financial Protection Bureau, "CFPB Takes Action Against Dwolla for Misrepresenting Data Security Practices" (Mar. 2, 2016), *https://www.consumerfinance.gov/about-us/newsroom/cfpb-takes-action-against-dwolla-for-misrepresenting-data-security-pract/*.

[56] Marc Rotenberg, "The Use of the Social Security Number as a National Identifier", 22 *Comp. & Soc'y* nos. 2, 3, 4 (Oct. 1991).

[57] Marc Rotenberg, Equifax, "The Credit Reporting Industry, And What Congress Should Do Next", *Harv. Bus. Rev.*, (Sep. 20, 2017).

security numbers of nearly half of all Americans were stolen. The solution is not, however, to replace the social security number with a national biometric identifier that raises serious privacy and security risks.[58] Instead, we suggest that the best way to minimize the problem of identity theft is to reduce the industry's reliance on the social security number as a personal identifier.[59] Congress should prohibit the use of the social security number in the private sector without explicit legal authorization.

D. Promote Innovative Technology To Minimize the Collection of Personal Data

The focus should now turn to how companies can minimize the collection of personal data and maximize consumer privacy and control. There are already initiatives to improve privacy protections in the field of data science, and these efforts could be adopted and further developed by the companies responsible for protecting consumer data.[60]

The newly formed Commission on Evidence-Based Policymaking recently issued a report that urged the adoption of privacy enhancement and preservation techniques, including "differential privacy" algorithms that can be used to glean information from data sets without revealing personal information.[61] We have also seen increasingly secure methods of two-factor authentication that can minimize the risk of phishing and other attempts to compromise personal data.[62] Even the consumer-facing financial companies are beginning to develop better mechanisms to enable control and monitoring of accounts, including dedicated applications to limit unauthorized debit card charges.[63] These are the techniques that Equifax and other credit reporting agencies should invest in to limit harm to consumers going forward.

E. Enact Baseline Privacy Legislation and Establish a Data Protection Agency

We have urged for many years that the United States update its privacy laws to address the challenges posed by new technologies and new business practices. The United States was once a leader and innovator in privacy protection, but we have now fallen behind many other countries that are seeking to ensure that the rapid adoption of new technologies does not leave them vulnerable to data breach, identity theft, and cyberattack. Certainly, the United States needs to do more.

A good starting point would be to enact the Consumer Privacy Bill of Rights, baseline privacy legislation that would put the responsibilities on companies that collect and use personal data to protect the information they choose to collect. The Consumer Privacy Bill of Rights follows the structure of many privacy laws in the United States and elsewhere. That means it could both harmonize and simplify compliance, and the CPBR could help resolve pending trade disputes with Europe and others about the protections for transborder data flows.

The United States should also establish as Data Protection Agency as has virtually every other advanced economy facing the challenges of the digital age. The current agencies in the United States tasked with protecting consumers and citizens lack the authority and even the personnel to do what needs to be done.

I am aware that these are ambitious recommendations and reach beyond the immediate concerns before this Committee. But U.S. consumers, businesses, and the U.S. Government face a genuine threat from the unbounded collection of personal data without adequate legal and technical protections. This data is now the target of foreign adversaries. Two years ago it was the OPM breach. Now it is the Equifax

---

[58] EPIC, "Identity Theft", *http://epic.org/privacy/idtheft/* (last visited October 13, 2017).

[59] "Cybersecurity and Data Protection in the Financial Services Sector", Hearing Before the H. Comm. on Fin. Servs., 112th Cong. (2011) (statement of Marc Rotenberg, Exec. Dir., EPIC), *https://financialservices.house.gov/uploadedfiles/091411rotenberg.pdf.*

[60] See, e.g., Comm. on Nat'l Statistics, Div. of Behavioral and Social Sciences and Education, Nat'l Academies of Science, Engineering, and Medicine, "Combining Data Sources While Protecting Privacy" (National Academies Press 2017); Cynthia Dwork and Aaron Roth, "The Algorithmic Foundations of Differential Privacy", 9 *Found. & Trends in Theoretical Comp. Sci.* 211 (2014).

[61] Marc Rotenberg, "Let's Use Government Data To Make Better Policy", *Sci. Am.* (Oct. 4, 2017), *https://blogs.scientificamerican.com/observations/let-rsquo-s-use-government-data-to-make-better-policy/.*

[62] See Letter from Sen. Ron Wyden (D-Ore.), Ranking Member, Comm. on Finance, to Acting Commissioner Nancy A. Berryhill, Social Sec'y Admin. (Oct. 5, 2017) (recommending the use of Universal Second Factor (U2F) tokens to secure social security accounts), *https://www.finance.senate.gov/imo/media/doc/100517%20RW%20to%20SSA%20U2F.pdf.*

[63] See, e.g., Ally Card Controls App (2017) (providing consumers with a way to "turn off" their debit card whenever they are not using it), *https://www.ally.com/help/bank/card-controls-app.html.* Debit cards pose an acute risk to consumers because consumers are not as well protected from fraudulent charges as they are with credit cards. See U.S. PIRG, Debit Card Facts, *http://www.pirg.org/consumer/banks/debit/debitcards1.htm* (last accessed Oct. 13, 2017).

breach. I am reluctant to imagine the consequences for the United States of the next major breach.

Conclusion

We think it is time now to reform the credit reporting industry and to end the practice of building massive, secretive, profiles on American consumers that are sold to strangers and obtained by hackers, yet are almost impossible for consumers to see or control.

EPIC supports legislation that will give consumers control over their information and establish accountability for companies in the personal data industry. EPIC also support techniques that minimize the collection of personally identifiable information. And we urge the end to the use of the SSN by private companies without legal authority.

It will come as no surprise that consumers across the country favor reform of the credit reporting industry. But I want to end with a story that may be surprising. Earlier this fall, I had the opportunity to speak with leading CEOs from across the country about the Equifax breach. After a brief exchange, the event moderator polled the CEOs. Eighty-seven percent said "the Equifax boss should go" and 95 percent "want stronger consumer privacy laws." [64]

American consumers favor stronger consumer privacy laws. American businesses favor stronger consumer privacy laws. Now it is time for Congress to Act.

Thank you for the opportunity to testify today. I will be pleased to answer your questions.

———

PREPARED STATEMENT OF CHRIS JAIKARAN

ANALYST IN CYBERSECURITY POLICY, CONGRESSIONAL RESEARCH SERVICE

OCTOBER 17, 2017

Introduction

Chairman Crapo, Ranking Member Brown, and Members of the Committee, thank you for the opportunity to testify on consumer data security and the credit bureaus. My name is Chris Jaikaran and I am an Analyst in Cybersecurity Policy at the Congressional Research Service. In this role, I research and analyze cybersecurity issues and their policy implications—including issues of data security, protection and management.

My testimony today will include discussion of data security as an element of cybersecurity and risk management, analysis and a case study on how data breaches occur, a description of cyberincident response, and possible options for Congress to address data security and data protection. My testimony today is based solely on publicly available information and CRS analysis.

Cybersecurity and Data Security

An increasingly used catch-phrase among industry analysts is that today "all companies are technology companies," or "all companies are data companies." [1] This concept reflects the role that information technology (IT) and data play in enabling the modern business practices that allow companies to compete and thrive in the marketplace. This reliance on IT and data also creates risk for corporate leadership to manage. Adequately controlling that risk is an objective of cybersecurity. [2]

Data security is an element of cybersecurity. At the most basic level, cybersecurity is the security of cyberspace, which includes not just data, but the networks, hardware, software, services, and infrastructure that data relies upon. It is also important to note that data does not exist by itself, but is created, manipulated and used by people. Consequently, cybersecurity is not just the security of data, hardware, software, infrastructure, networks and services—but also the human users of cyberspace.

Computer scientists view data security through three attributes:

---

[64] CEO Summit, Chief Executive Leadership Institute, Yale School of Management, Washington, DC (Sept. 9, 2017), *http://som.yale.edu/faculty-research-centers/centers-initiatives/chief-executive-leadership-institute/programs/ceo-summit.*

[1] Nathaniel Fink, "Cybersecurity for a New America: What's Next for the Cybersecurity Community", conference keynote, March 20, 2017, at *https://youtu.be/wfMpUpxNPAg.* Avi Gesser, Gabriel Rosenberg, and Matt Kelly, "Cybersecurity and Data Management", webinar, Davis Polk & Wardwell LLP, October 11, 2017.

[2] Risk may be managed by avoiding the risk, controlling the risk, transferring the risk, or accepting the risk. DHS Risk Steering Committee, "DHS Risk Lexicon", report, September 2010, at *https://www.dhs.gov/sites/default/files/publications/dhs-risk-lexicon-2010l0.pdf.*

- *Confidentiality:* that the data is only known to authorized parties. A data breach is an example of how confidentiality is breached, while encryption is a tool used to ensure confidentiality.
- *Integrity:* that the data is known to the authorized parties as intended. Data manipulation is an example of how integrity is breached, while there are data checking technologies, such as blockchain, to ensure that one can verify the integrity of data.
- *Availability:* that the data is available to authorized parties when they choose. Ransomware attacks availability, while backups are a tool that ensures availability of data.

Related to integrity is the concept of authentication, an attribute that one can verify that data is from a trusted source. The Internet was built using technologies that assumed the trust of its users, but as the Internet has grown into a global network, anonymity and the manipulation of data have proliferated. [3]

As an element of cybersecurity, data security involves risk management. Absolute security is not obtainable, so managing the risks which would impair security is generally considered to be the goal. In order to evaluate risk, managers need to understand the threats the enterprises may face, the vulnerabilities the enterprise has, and the consequences of an incident. [4]

Threats are generally considered to be the gamut of potential human attackers. Such attackers include Nation-State actors, criminals and insiders to the network. Depending on the data an entity houses, and the services it provides, the realm of attackers may change from one day to the next, sometimes even driven by events in the news.

Vulnerabilities exist in software the moment it is shipped to users. Adding additional software to a growing enterprise creates complexities that can lead to further potential vulnerabilities. Some software vulnerabilities are known the day they are shipped and are catalogued in the Common Vulnerabilities and Exposures database with risk assessments enumerated in the National Vulnerabilities Database. [5] Others are discovered later. Vulnerabilities that are discovered but not disclosed to the vendor so they may be patched are called 0-days (zero or "oh" days). However, 0-day vulnerabilities do not necessarily create a large risk for enterprises. In addition to a vulnerability being present on a system, it must be exploited to cause some impact. The exploitation of a vulnerability may be so difficult that an entity's risk of falling victim to that 0-day is low. Despite 0-days being a threat, most cybersecurity incidents occur through attackers exploiting known vulnerabilities for which the entity has not deployed a patch. [6]

Consequences may vary based on the business of an entity, the data that entity houses, and the stakeholder community for the entity. Consequences are also multi-dimensional. The loss of data may inhibit business practices, but may also lead to reputational loss, enforcement actions, payments to stakeholders, or other impacts.

An entity may be able to better predict consequences through understanding the data in its possession. Using a data model or framework can help an entity identify attributes of its data. Such attributes include: where data is acquired; what other data the entity generates from acquired data; what types (both descriptively and by file type) of data is acquired or generated; how the entity will use and access data; how the data will be shared with other parties; where data is stored, accessed, and transmitted; and what policies exist for data retention and data disposal. Such a data model is essentially an architecture of the entity's data, similar to the network architecture of their IT systems or the blueprints for their building.

The National Institute of Standards and Technology (NIST) *Framework for Improving Critical Infrastructure Cybersecurity* (Framework) provides functions, activities and categories in a common format to assist entities in thinking through cybersecurity issues and identifying resources to assist in completing activities. [7] (Some of these activities include asset management, data security, and detection processes.) However, the Cybersecurity Framework is not the only reference for organizations to consider using, or a document which they can only use exclusively. The Center for Internet Security, the International Standards Organization, and ISACA

---

[3] CRS In Focus IF10559, *Cybersecurity: An Introduction*, by Chris Jaikaran.

[4] Davis Hake, "Threat, Vulnerability, Consequence", interview with *The Cipher Brief*, December 15, 2015, at *https://www.thecipherbrief.com/threat-vulnerability-consequence*.

[5] *https://cve.mitre.org.; https://nvd.nist.gov.*

[6] Jory Heckman, "Hackers Not Yet Pulling Out Big Guns for Data Breaches, NSA Official Warns", Federal News Radio article, October 18, 2016, at *https://federalnewsradio.com/technology/2016/10/hackers-not-yet-pulling-big-guns-data-breaches-nsa-official-warns/*.

[7] NIST, "Cybersecurity Framework", webpage, at *https://www.nist.gov/cyberframework*.

also publish cybersecurity frameworks which an entity may use in conjunction with or in replacement of the NIST Cybersecurity Framework.[8]

The Anatomy of a Breach

The recent breach of Equifax provides a timely case study on how breaches occur.[9] While a single command may be executed at a speed fast enough for the computer to process it, full attacks are done by humans, and as such, occur at human speed. Breaches can be understood through an attack framework.[10]

First, an attacker examines the target. Through this examination the attacker learns about the target system. This examination is both online and off. Business cards provide the naming convention for user accounts on the system (in the form of email addresses), while digital tools can provide information on services running on Internet-facing services. In the case of Equifax, scans of their credit report dispute website may discover that Apache Struts was an available service and that it was running under a vulnerable version.[11]

Second, an attacker exploits a vulnerability. This initial exploitation provides the entryway for an attacker into the system or network. As stated earlier, vulnerabilities themselves do not necessarily create a significant risk scenario for an enterprise, but an exploitation of that vulnerability may. In some cases, a single vulnerability is required to gain access, while in others multiple vulnerabilities may be used to create an effective exploit. In the case of Equifax, a vulnerability in an earlier version of Apache Struts allowed for remote code execution.[12] NIST deemed this type of vulnerability as critical, and the Apache Foundation patched it and provided an additional work around.[13] At the time it was patched, it was also added to penetration testing software so that system administrators could test to see if they were still vulnerable to exploitation.[14]

Third, after the initial exploitation, attackers entrench into the system. By entrenching into a system, attackers are discovering more about the network they have penetrated. In this phase, they gain access to additional systems in that network, escalate their privileges so that they have further access, and acquire additional credentials. In the case of Equifax, how attackers entrenched into the system is publicly unknown. However, many instances of Apache Struts run on web servers with default administrative credentials, which may have provided the next step for an attacker to entrench into the system.[15]

While he was the Chief of the National Security Agency's Tailored Access Operations unit, current White House Cybersecurity Coordinator Rob Joyce said that "you know the things you intend to have in your network, we look for the things that are actually in your network."[16] This summarizes the relationship between defenders and attackers. Defenders know what they acquired, deployed and intend to have on their network, while attackers know the vulnerabilities and what else is running on that network. Exploiting vulnerabilities and entrenching into systems takes advantage of this asymmetric knowledge.

---

[8] Cybersecurity frameworks from these organizations can be found at *https://www.cisecurity.org/controls/*; *https://www.iso.org/standard/54533.html;* and *http://www.isaca.org/cobit/pages/default.aspx.* ISACA was previously known as the Information Systems Audit and Control Association, but now goes by its acronym only.

[9] Information on the Equifax breach is derived from testimony provided by former CEO Richard Smith before the U.S. Senate Committee on Banking, Housing, and Urban Affairs. Richard Smith, "Prepared Testimony of Richard Smith", testimony, October 4, 2017, at *https://www.banking.senate.gov/public/—cache/files/da2d3277-d6f4-493a-ad88-c809781f7011/F143CC8431E6CD31C86ADB64041FB31B.smith-testimony-10-4-17.pdf.*

[10] The framework presented in this testimony is based on previous analysis by CRS. Further case studies are available via CRS Recorded Event WRE00157, "Cybersecurity: Anatomy of a Breach", by Chris Jaikaran.

[11] Apache Struts is a developer framework which allows for common programming languages, such as Java, to be used to develop user facing web applications. It is open source software maintained by the Apache Software Foundation, *https://struts.apache.org/.*

[12] CVE, "CVE-2017-5638", data base entry, at *https://cve.mitre.org/cgi-bin/cvename.cgi?name=CVE-2017-5638.*

[13] NIST, "CVE-201705638 Detail", webpage, March 10, 2017, at *https://nvd.nist.gov/vuln/detail/CVE-2017-5638.* Apache Foundation, "S2-045," webpage, at *https://struts.apache.org/docs/s2-045.html.*

[14] The exploitation of CVE-2017-5638 was added to the Metasploit Framework. *https://github.com/rapid7/metasploit-framework/issues/8064.*

[15] Hector Monsegur, "How To Fight Hackers, With Former Black-Hat Hacker Hector Monsegur", podcast, October 2, 2017, at *https://lifehacker.com/how-to-protect-yourself-from-hackers-with-hector-monse-1819075906.*

[16] Rob Joyce, "USENIX Enigma 2016—NSA TAO Chief on Disrupting Nation State Hackers", conference talk, January 28, 2016, at *https://www.youtube.com/watch?v=bDJb8WOJYdA.*

Fourth, after gaining access, attackers can then execute steps to achieve their objectives. These objectives could be to compromise the confidentiality of the data by stealing it. Confidentiality is not only compromised by theft, but also by access. This distinction is referred to as exposure versus exfiltration. Data is exposed when an unauthorized party may access it on an entity's network, but it is exfiltrated when they take it off that network. This relationship is akin to perusing books in a library but only checking out one. All the books are exposed to a patron, but only the borrowed book is exfiltrated. The integrity of data may be compromised by altering the data in a system. Alternatively, the availability of the data may be compromised by deleting it or otherwise making it unavailable (e.g., through encrypting data in a ransomware attack). In the case of Equifax, it appears that over 145 million people had their data exposed, while some had their dispute documents (which contain personally identifiable information) and credit card information exfiltrated.

Finally, the attackers would exit on their terms. After achieving their objectives, the attackers would seek to leave the system so that they may have access again at a later date, or to cover evidence of their activities. Deleting log files, adding connections to network whitelists and creating credentials are examples of activities an attacker would undergo to exit the compromised system on their terms. In the case of Equifax, it is unknown from publicly available sources what attackers did in this phase.

By understanding how attacks occur through such a framework, system defenders could develop defense-in-depth strategies to mitigate breaches. Defense-in-depth is an approach which uses layered countermeasures to defend against cybersecurity risks throughout a network. [17] Countermeasures could be layered to address each phase of an attack so that defenders are quickly alerted to attacks and can take actions to prevent further damage to their enterprise.

Cybersecurity Incident Response

Cybersecurity incident response describes when system administrators seek to confirm the attack, discover information about it, and mitigate against it. The response as described below is from the breached entity's perspective, and does not discuss Government response options.

Incident response is not limited to the time immediately following an attack, however. Before an attack, response planning, training, and exercising can occur. Response planning helps an organization think though its risks and how it will respond to those risks, train its personnel on how to respond to attacks, and practice its response to build confidence in staff and management as to the organization's capability and capacity to manage incidents.

For incident response, staff is not limited to just IT personnel. Response planning should also include, among others, communications staff that are able to craft messages to both internal and external stakeholders, legal teams who can help with reporting and compliance requirements, and management and corporate boards who are accountable for the operations of a corporation.

There will be a delay between the discovery of an attack and public notification of that attack because analysis of what transpired will need to be conducted. This analysis will inform the entity of how they were breached and what data or systems were compromised. This type of analysis may be conducted by the entity itself, a business partner of the entity, Government response teams and law enforcement. With a variety of potential forensic investigators, determining how they will coordinate in their response and how they will share information among one another is a factor that can be determined during the planning and training phase. With information on how the breach happened and the extent of the breach, the entity can proceed to mitigate its affects. These two phases need not occur in succession, but may be able to occur concurrently.

Finally, the organization can improve their data security and response planning by learning from their efforts and applying insights gained.

Potential Options for Congress

Three options for Congress are presented below to generate discussion. They are not recommendations from CRS. Given time constraints, these options are provided with limited policy discussion and are not exhaustive.

---

[17] Industrial Control Systems Cyber Emergency Response Team, "Recommended Practice: Improving Industrial Control System Cybersecurity with Defense-in-Depth Strategies", report, September 2016, at *https://ics-cert.us-cert.gov/sites/default/files/recommended\practices/NCCIC\ICS-CERT\Defense\in\Depth\2016\S508C.pdf.*

Authorize a Federal Agency To Examine for Information Security

Congress can authorize a Federal agency to engage in supervisory examinations of the credit reporting agencies (CRAs) for compliance with the safeguards rule. [18]

As an example, the Consumer Financial Protection Board (CFPB) has broad authority to bring enforcement cases against corporations for unfair and deceptive business practices. CRS research could not identify an enforcement case or issued guidance where CFPB sought to address information security. This may be because CFPB has an express prohibition against issuing rules concerning information security and bringing enforcement actions against an entity concerning information security. Instead, the authority to issue a standard for the protection of nonpublic personal information, and enforce that standard, is retained by the Federal Trade Commission (FTC). [19] The FTC issued the safeguards rule in 2002 pursuant to the authority referenced above and is currently seeking public comment on an update. [20]

Instead of engaging with CRAs after a cybersecurity incident, CFPB has the authority to supervise CRAs prior to an incident occurring. [21] Congress could explicitly authorize CFPB to examine CRAs for their adherence to the safeguards rule, as promulgated by the FTC. The dialogue created by CFPB and a CRA could lead to greater understanding of the cybersecurity risk faced by the CRAs and allow CRAs with deficiencies to correct their data security measures prior to referral to FTC for enforcement action. As this is not an activity CFPB currently engages in during an examination, a new program may need to be established in the CFPB to recruit the talent to manage such a technical examination. [22]

Regulate Personal Data Collection and Use

Congress could regulate the collection, use, and retention of data regardless of the type of entity housing that data. The European Union has such a regulation known as the General Data Protection Regulation (GDPR), and Canada is in the process of updating their Personal Information Protection and Electronics Document Act (PIPEDA). [23] In proactively regulating data, Congress can establish data use requirements. Some of those requirements may include what data may be collected, how data must be stored (e.g., encryption, location, etc.), the consumer's rights to collection and use of data about them, and under which circumstances data may be shared with other parties. While the United States does not have an overarching law governing data use, U.S. agencies have promulgated guidance on data protection. [24]

Require Data Transparency

Congress could require CRAs, or any entity that profits from consumer data, to identify and disclose their data model to consumers. Disclosure of all elements of the model may not be necessary (i.e., where data is stored). However, some elements such as where data is acquired, how it is used, and what other data the entity generates about the consumer may provide consumers with additional information and affect their decisions in the marketplace. For example, if a consumer knew that a CRA acquired data from a company they have a business relationship with, they may choose to limit their interactions with that company or seek out an opt-out/opt-in form from that business to limit how their data may be shared.

Conclusion

Thank you for the opportunity to testify today. I look forward to your questions. If you require further analysis of these options, or other policy issues before Congress, my colleagues and I at the CRS stand ready to assist you.

---

[18] 16 CFR §314

[19] 15 U.S.C. §6801, §6804, §6805.

[20] 16 CFR §314. *https://www.ftc.gov/enforcement/rules/rulemaking-regulatory-reform-proceedings/safeguards-rule.*

[21] 12 U.S.C. §5514.

[22] Current CFPB examination procedures may be found online at *https://www.consumerfinance.gov/policy-compliance/guidance/supervision-examinations/.*

[23] *http://www.eugdpr.org/; https://www.priv.gc.ca/en/privacy-topics/privacy-laws-in-canada/the-personal-information-protection-and-electronic-documents-act-pipeda/.*

[24] FTC, "Protecting Personal Information", guide, October 2016, at *https://www.ftc.gov/system/files/documents/plain-language/pdf-0136lproteting-personal-information.pdf.*

RESPONSES TO WRITTEN QUESTIONS OF CHAIRMAN CRAPO FROM ANDREW M. SMITH

Q.1. What is the most effective action a consumer can take to protect against identity theft if the consumer's information has been compromised? Please include a detailed description of the differences between credit freezes, credit locks, and fraud alerts, including how long each takes to activate and de-activate and the relative benefits and drawbacks of each.

A.1. There are many ways for consumers to protect themselves if they believe that they may be at risk of identity theft. The first step is to check credit card statements and free credit reports for charges and accounts that are unfamiliar. Consumers should also consider placing an initial fraud alert, an extended fraud alert and, if in the military, a military alert. Consumers should also consider engaging a credit monitoring service—there are a number of free services available.

Freezes are another option, though they may not be the best choice for many consumers. Although credit freezes may seem like a good idea in the abstract, for those who may become credit active they could be a problem. Press stories [1] have recently noted that some with credit freezes have missed out on opportunities because they had a credit freeze.

If a consumer nonetheless chooses a freeze, all three national credit bureaus offer freezes to consumers regardless of their place of residence. Freezes are free for victims of identity theft and minors who have a credit file.

A lock is intended to work similarly to a credit freeze. Consumers who place freezes do so in order to ensure that no new credit can be offered without their explicit agreement, and a lock will achieve that consumer goal, but will be much easier for consumers to use, as it will be app-based and occur in real time. By contrast, freezes are State-regulated and are generally PIN-based systems.

Legally, there are important differences between locks and freezes. Freezes are State-mandated products that are heavily regulated. In many States PINs are mandated as authentication, and if a consumer has the PIN, the freeze can be lifted almost immediately. If the consumer has lost the PIN, however, it can take days for a new PIN to be mailed to a consumer's address and for the consumer to again contact the company.

Lock products, by contrast, are not State-mandated products and require consumers to enter into a formal business relationship with the company. This is an important distinction between the two products.

For the consumer, the lock will deliver the same functionality as a freeze, but do so in a less cumbersome fashion.

Q.2. Are credit bureaus required to provide data to any Federal agency? If so, is it mandated or at the request of the regulator; what data is provided; what agency is it provided to; and is the data sold or provided for free?

---

[1] See, e.g.: *http://appleinsider.com/articles/17/10/27/iphone-x-orders-held-up-by-credit-freezes-put-in-place-after-equifax-hack* and *http://sanfrancisco.cbslocal.com/2017/09/14/apple-iphone-x-equifax-data-breach-credit-freeze/*.

A.2. CRAs are only able to deliver data for permissible purposes as defined in Section 604 of the Fair Credit Reporting Act. There are a number of legitimate Government purposes for obtaining credit reports, including benefit eligibility and child support enforcement.

Some agencies of the U.S. Government purchase aggregated, anonymized data from our companies for market monitoring and research purposes. This information is not regulated under the Fair Credit Reporting Act because it is not identifiable to any specific individual.

Credit bureaus are required to provide credit report information to Government agencies for counterterrorism purposes and to the FBI for counterintelligence purposes, upon an appropriate certification from the agency. These provisions were added to the FCRA by the USA PATRIOT Act and 2001. We are not aware of any other provisions requiring credit bureaus to provide credit report information to Government agencies.

Q.3. Many States have laws requiring credit bureaus to provide credit freezes. Can you describe what these laws generally require and discuss whether it is appropriate for Congress to create a Federal standard?

A.3. All 50 States have credit freeze laws and while there are a number of similarities, there are enough variations among the States that a Federal standard on credit freezes would equalize treatment of these important products across the country, offering certainty to a mobile population.

––––––

RESPONSES TO WRITTEN QUESTIONS OF SENATOR BROWN FROM ANDREW M. SMITH

Q.1. In your testimony, you claimed that consumer reporting agencies charge for security freezes due to a "patchwork of laws." This statement seems to imply that State laws require consumer reporting agencies to charge for security freezes. But isn't it true that State laws generally cap the fees that consumer reporting agencies can charge for security freezes (i.e., they set a ceiling, not a floor)? Ohio law, for example, provides that a consumer reporting agency "may" charge a fee for placing, removing, or temporarily lifting a fee. See Ohio Rev. Code §1349.52(I). Is it your position that Ohio's and other States' laws nevertheless require consumer reporting agencies to charge fees for security freezes?

A.1. It is not our position that the Ohio law requires consumer reporting agencies to charge a fee for security freezes. However, in most cases, the credit bureaus have good reason to charge a fee, a fact that State legislators have recognized in explicitly permitting the bureaus to charge such a fee. Credit bureaus are not the breached entity in most cases [1] and they should not be forced to pay to absorb the costs of a breach caused by someone else. In other cases, States do not require service providers to pay for crimi-

––––––

[1] The largest breaches in history have been, in numerical order of consumers affected, Yahoo!, Adult Friend Finder, eBay, Equifax, Heartland Payment Systems, Target, TJX (TJ Maxx), JP Morgan, U.S. Office of Personnel Management, and Sony's PlayStation Network. Taylor Armeding, "The 16 Biggest Data Breaches of the 21st Century", CSO, Oct. 11, 2017, *https:// www.csoonline.com/article/2130877/data-breach/the-16-biggest-data-breaches-of-the-21st-century.html.*

nal activity unrelated to their service, for example: States do not require a burglar alarm company to give away services for thefts in a neighborhood.

For victims of identity theft, consumers in every State are entitled to free credit freezes. The freeze fee is low and allows credit bureaus to recover some of the costs for providing freezes. This service is not a profit center for any company. The administrative fee instead helps to cover the costs of providing the freeze service to consumers, including the maintenance of the technology to implement the freeze system.

Q.2. Although Equifax has offered a free security freeze in the wake of the breach, other consumer reporting agencies have refused to offer a free security freeze. Will Consumer Data Industry Association (CDIA) members other than Equifax offer a free security freeze or will they only do it if required by law to do so?

A.2. The consumer reporting agencies that were not the subject of a hack or a breach will continue to charge non-ID theft victims for credit freezes as permitted by law. Identity theft victims are entitled to free freezes. As noted, the administrative fees for credit freezes help to cover the costs of providing the freeze service to consumers, including the development and maintenance of the technology to implement the freeze system and the consumer counseling required to explain the freeze and how to manage the freeze.

Q.3. To purchase products like credit monitoring from consumer reporting agencies, consumers frequently must sign forced-arbitration clauses in fine print. In your testimony, you implied that these forced-arbitration clauses apply only to disputes related to the products that consumers are purchasing. But many consumer reporting agencies' forced-arbitration clauses would appear to cover claims beyond just these products. For example, Equifax's forced-arbitration clause provides that "[a]ny Claim . . . raised by either [the consumer] or Equifax against the other shall be subject to mandatory, binding arbitration." The clause defines "Claim" as meaning "any claim, dispute, or controversy between [the consumer] and [Equifax] relating in any way to [the consumer's] relationship with Equifax." Likewise, one of Experian's forced-arbitration clauses extends to "all disputes and claims between [the consumer and Experian], except any disputes or claims which under governing law are not subject to arbitration." TransUnion has a similarly broad forced-arbitration clause, and all three companies deprive consumers of their rights to band together in class actions. Is it your legal opinion that these clauses nevertheless cover only disputes related to the specific products that consumers are purchasing?

A.3. A legal opinion on the specifics of the three nationwide credit bureaus' arbitration clauses and the scope of those clauses are best left to the companies offering those clauses.

Q.4. During the hearing, I asked you to tell the consumer reporting agencies that you represent that there is strong sentiment that they should not include forced-arbitration clauses in their credit-lock products. What message did you convey to them? If there is written correspondence, please provide a copy of that correspondence for the record. Please also provide any response by the consumer reporting agencies or their representatives.

A.4. I have notified the U.S. General Counsel at Equifax, Experian, and TransUnion that you have asked me to convey to them your concerns regarding arbitration clauses. My message was as follows: "In the October 17 Senate Banking Committee hearing on credit bureaus and data security, Senator Brown asked me to convey to the three nationwide consumer reporting agencies that "there is strong sentiment" that consumer reporting agencies should not include forced arbitration clauses in their credit lock products." They have confirmed receipt of my message.

Q.5. In your testimony, you stated that forced-arbitration clauses play a "special role" with respect to credit-monitoring and other credit-report-related products because of the "exigent circumstance" created by the Credit Repair Organizations Act's "stringent penalties." As you know, Congress passed this Act after finding that certain business practices of credit repair organizations had "worked a financial hardship upon consumers, particularly those of limited economic means and who are inexperienced in credit matters." Thus, "to protect the public from unfair or deceptive advertising and business practices" by these organizations, Congress allowed consumers to recover compensation for harm caused by the organizations' deceptive conduct. In your opinion, could any of the three national consumer reporting agencies' use their force-arbitration clauses to legally block consumers from banding together in class actions to sue under the Credit Repair Organizations Act?

A.5. The Credit Repair Organizations Act (CROA) was never intended to apply to credit bureaus, which are heavily regulated by the FCRA, yet some courts have not correctly interpreted CROA. This misapplication of law is why credit bureaus feel compelled to provide arbitration clauses, and it is why we have urged Congress to amend CROA. I have attached an April 14, 2017, letter from CDIA to Chairman Crapo and Ranking Member Brown where CDIA advocated for, among other things, Congressional assistance to amend CROA.

In short, the broad definitions in CROA have labeled traditional consumer reporting agencies as CROs, subjecting consumer reporting agencies to CROA's strict liability provisions when they seek to offer legitimate credit education services to consumers.

Misinterpretation of CROA by the courts has stretched the law beyond Congressional intent of combatting fraudulent credit repair practices. Recent judicial decisions have even swept in standard credit monitoring services and identity theft protection services, as well as other credit education services that consumers seek.[2] This expansion has deterred trusted companies from providing legitimate credit education products to consumers, including innovative credit simulators that help consumers understand personalized steps to improve their credit scores. If CROA remains unchanged, consumers are effectively prevented from accessing these tools.

Q.6. In your testimony, you implied that if Americans had the right to make consumer reporting agencies delete their data, consumers

---

[2] See, Stout v. FreeScore, 743 F.3d 680 (9th Cir. 2014).

would use this right to "selectively delete" negative but accurate information. Do any CDIA members operate in countries whose laws provide for a "right of erasure" similar to the right that exists under the EU General Data Protection Regulation (GDPR)? If so, please provide (1) concrete, credible examples of instances where consumers have exercised this right to selectively delete negative but accurate credit information from CDIA members' files and (2) the total number of such instances reported and confirmed in 2016 (by country). In each case, please include only those instances for which you can confirm the accuracy of the information that the consumer sought to delete.

A.6. When a consumer has the ability to selectively delete the parts of their credit history that are accurate but derogatory, the entire credit system suffers and safety and soundness of the financial system is jeopardized. It is hard to imagine a credit system where a consumer can delete late payments and keep only on time payment history. Full file reporting is a value supported by credit bureaus, lenders, and the prudential regulators.

In 1999, several Federal banking regulators took note that some national financial institutions were not fully reporting data to consumer reporting agencies. In response to this situation, the Comptroller of the Currency called this a "particularly objectionable practice". This "[f]ailure to report may not be explicitly illegal[, b]ut it can be readily characterized as unfair; it may well be deceptive, and—in any context—it's abusive."[3]

Similarly, under EU law, the "right to be forgotten" does not actually grant consumers the power to selectively delete information from their credit report. The "right to be forgotten" will not override the legitimate interest financial entities and CRAs have to share a complete and accurate credit file. In these respects, the credit reporting systems in the EU work remarkably similarly to the credit reporting system in the U.S. under the Fair Credit Reporting Act. The GDPR recognizes that a fair, affordable and efficient credit market demands accurate reporting of debts and payment histories to and from CRAs. The tenets of legitimate interest are balanced by providing transparency and access for consumers with their right to challenge and correct inaccurate information.

Although there may be some temporary confusion about how the GDPR will work with respect to consumer consent for credit reference agencies (CRAs) to collect information from lenders, and the "right to be forgotten" or right of erasure, CDIA members do not anticipate material changes to the way credit reporting currently works in the majority of EU countries as a result of GDPR.

GDPR provides for six bases by which information can be processed, consent being only one of them. In the context of credit reporting, the relevant basis for information processing is the "legitimate interest" of the data processor.

In the U.K., the Information Commissioners Office (ICO), the Government agency that interprets and enforces GDPR in the U.K., has already provided written guidance that consumer consent

---

[3] Remarks by John D. Hawke, Comptroller of the Currency, before a conference sponsored by the Consumer Bankers Association, San Francisco, California, June 7, 1999. See also, Federal Financial Institutions Examination Council Advisory Letter to Chief Executive Officers regarding Consumer Credit Reporting Practices, Jan. 18, 2000.

is not needed for sharing of credit information with CRAs. The ICO has said that both lenders and CRAs in the U.K. can rely upon the basis of "legitimate interest" for the sharing of credit data, and that the consent of the consumer is not needed under GDPR.

Similarly, the "right to be forgotten" will not over-ride the legitimate interest financial entities and CRAs have to share a complete and accurate credit file. In these respects, the credit reporting systems in the EU work similarly to the credit reporting system in the U.S. under the Fair Credit Reporting Act. The Europeans have learned of the importance of a robust credit reporting system from the U.S. experience, and the GDPR appropriately recognizes that a fair, affordable and efficient credit market demands accurate reporting of debts and payment histories to and from CRAs. The tenets of legitimate interest are balanced by providing transparency and access for consumers, as well as a right to challenge and correct inaccurate information.

The inability of lenders to fully understand credit risk associated with the extension of consumer loans would negatively affect the price and availability of credit in the EU and introduce systemic risk into the banking systems of individual country and EU banking systems. Therefore, in the context of credit reporting, the legitimate interests of financial institutions to understand an individual's credit risk outweighs an individual's right to be forgotten.

Q.7. For each of the three national consumer reporting agencies, please provide a list of all EU countries (including the United Kingdom) in which the company or any of its affiliates operates. For each agency—country combination, please list the applicable division or business unit's revenue, operating income, and operating margin (each according to generally accepted accounting principles). Additionally, for each agency—country combination, please state whether the agency intends to withdraw from the country when the new GDPR (or its U.K. equivalent) goes into effect.

A.7. Based on information provided by the three nationwide credit bureaus, we can relay the following information:

Trans Union does not operate any consumer credit reporting businesses in any EU countries and does not realize any revenue or income from consumer credit reporting activities in any EU countries.

Experian Operates consumer credit bureaus in the following EU countries:

Country	Annual Revenues FY2017	Operating Income FY2017	Operating Margin FY2017
United Kingdom & Ireland	$807,400,000	$245,900,000	30.55%
Other EU Countries: Italy, Spain, Denmark, Netherlands	$96,100,000	$20,900,000	25.04%

Equifax operates in the following EU countries:

Country	Annual Revenues FY2017	Operating Income FY2017	Operating Margin FY2017
United Kingdom	$156,200,000	$27,700,000	17.7%
Spain	$42,500,000	$8,800,000	20.7%
Ireland	-	($2,000,000)	N/A
Portugal	$600,000	$0	-1.0%

Neither Experian nor Equifax intends to withdraw from any country in which it operates consumer credit bureaus when the new GDPR or its equivalent goes into effect in May 2018.

Q.8. Please describe, in concrete terms, the actions that CDIA members operating in the European Union (including the United Kingdom) are taking to comply with the GDPR (or its U.K. equivalent), including how they plan to accommodate the right of erasure.

A.8. For this answer, we have asked the three major credit bureaus to respond directly.

Answer from Experian:

Experian is currently engaged to ensure they are in compliance with the GDPR in each country in which they operate at the time the GDPR becomes effective in May 2018. This effort includes a review and, where necessary, changes to Experian's guidelines, policies and practices relating to our credit bureau operations in the EU.

Answer from Equifax:

Our current analysis indicates that Equifax's U.S. operations do not process data that is subject to the extraterritorial application of GDPR. As such, Equifax is taking measures to comply with its contractual obligations under data processing agreements with data controllers or processors that have indicated that the data they provide to Equifax for processing in the U.S. is subject to GDPR.

In the U.K., Equifax has been investing and working on its GDPR compliance project since 2016, including following the 12 step approach as outlined and promoted by the U.K. data protection regulator, the Information Commissioner's Office (ICO).

These actions include reviewing and updating (as appropriate) contractual arrangements with clients, suppliers and processors with up-to-date GDPR contractual terms and ensuring contractual terms include cooperation and assistance provisions between the parties so that Data Subject Rights (including the right of erasure) can be fulfilled where appropriate and required.

In addition, regarding the right of erasure, Equifax is working on a joint exercise with the other U.K. CRAs, the ICO and key financial services clients to implement a standard U.K. Credit Reference Agency Information Notice (CRAIN) that all credit data sharers must utilize in their interactions with their customers post-GDPR. This standard will ensure the ongoing, lawful sharing and processing of credit report information.

In Iberia, Equifax has also been working on its GDPR compliance project since 2016. In common with the U.K., this activity includes reviewing and updating (as appropriate) contractual arrangements with clients, suppliers and processors with up-to-date GDPR contractual terms. In addition to the requirements of the GDPR, a forthcoming Spanish data protection regulation will affect the business.

The review of operations includes the right of erasure in respect of both 'negative' (missed payments) and 'positive' bureau data, to which different procedures apply.

Equifax is taking the necessary steps toward achieving compliance with GDPR on or before the May 2018 deadline.

Q.9. Would there be any benefits from consistency between U.S. and EU privacy standards?

A.9. Each country's financial system is different, but the framework laid out in the Fair Credit Reporting Act has led to the most democratic and fair credit system in the world, and in so far as this being a goal, we would urge adoption of U.S. principles in Europe and across the world.

Q.10. In your testimony, you stated that consumers have access to "all of the information on file about them with consumer reporting agencies." But isn't it true that consumer reporting agencies or their affiliates often collect information that is not contained in the free annual credit reports that consumers can obtain? Please provide a list of all types of data collected by the three national consumer reporting agencies and their affiliates that is not contained in the free credit report that consumers can obtain under FCRA.

A.10. Federal law requires that consumer reporting agencies provide to consumers "All information in the consumer's file." [4] The definition of a "file" is quite broad and means "all of the information on that consumer recorded and retained by a consumer reporting agency regardless of how the information is stored." [5] under case law and FTC guidance, these definitions have been broadly interpreted to include information that might possibly be included in a consumer report about the subject consumer; this includes the identifying information on file with the credit bureau, a history of their payments on various credit lines and loans, and public record information, such as liens and judgements.

RESPONSES TO WRITTEN QUESTIONS OF SENATOR SCHATZ FROM ANDREW M. SMITH

Q.1. What is the cost to consumer reporting agencies to place security freezes on consumers' credit reports? Please compare that to the cost of providing consumers with the ability to "lock" and "unlock" their credit reports.

A.1. It is difficult to precisely measure the costs of providing security freezes, but the costs are certainly such that the three nationwide credit bureaus do not make a profit from their freeze obligations, even in those States where a fee is permitted.

Costs arise from a number of sources. Generally, CDIA members balance between limiting costs and investing in innovation in this space. In addition, different States have different requirements for placing security freezes on credit files. These laws require companies to maintain certain functionalities for consumers, including

---

[4] 15 U.S. Code §1681g.
[5] 15 U.S. Code §1681a(g).

training and maintaining call center employees. Other costs come from operating secure web channels and maintaining PINs for consumers. While most States allow for some cost recovery, as noted above, none of the three nationwide credit bureaus realize a profit on their security freeze obligations.

Furthermore, companies are investing significant resources into their credit lock options for consumers. In addition to significant development costs, there will be ongoing costs related to maintaining and upgrading secure systems. Despite the significant costs, we believe that the app-based systems meet consumer demand for more simplified interaction when setting and lifting a lock.

Q.2. Please explain how long it takes the consumer reporting agencies to process a request to freeze or unfreeze their credit report. Please explain how this length of time differs from the credit lock products that they offer, which enable consumers the ability to "lock" or "unlock" their credit reports instantaneously.

A.2. It depends through which channel a consumer request arrives. Most credit freeze laws require that a temporary lift of a freeze be completed within three business days of the request. Under most State freeze laws, if a consumer request comes through the internet or by phone, a temporary lift can be done within 15 minutes of the request, assuming the consumer provide the correct PIN.

A lock product assumes that a consumer has already been authenticated at the time an account was set up and therefore a lock/unlock can occur very quickly after a request is made. However, it is important to note that the account set-up will take some time as a consumer has to go through a number of steps to authenticate themselves to the CRA.

Q.3. Do you think consumers should be able to see the same credit report information that their bank uses when the bank makes a credit decision?

A.3. The information provided by a CRA to a lender under a permissible purpose is essentially the same as the information provided by a CRA to a consumer when the consumer requests his or her report. That information, however, is presented in different formats that are usable and understandable by each party. The information provided to a lender is presented in a computerized data feed not readable by a consumer, but the underlying information is the same as in a consumer file disclosure.

In addition, there might be differences due to the passage of time, or the identifying information provided by the lender to the consumer reporting agency to obtain a consumer report about the subject individual. The "same report" issues were studied by the FTC and the subject of a report to Congress in 2004 and what was true then remains true today. The FTC concluded that a same report requirement

> could impose substantial costs on both consumers and industry as a whole. The potential costs to consumers would include the privacy concerns raised by receiving a report that could pertain to another person. Further, if creditors were required to provide reports automatically with an "adverse action" notice, this could increase the volume of

reports being sent and thus raise identity theft concerns . . . To the extent that a consumer wanted to verify the accuracy of information currently in the file, the same report requirement would be less helpful because the "same report" would be somewhat out of date and perhaps incomplete. In contrast, consumer disclosures currently mandated under the FCRA provide all information about a consumer in the CRA's files at the time the consumer requests disclosure. A same report requirement could thus indirectly impose additional costs on consumers attempting to identify and correct information currently contained in their reports. [7]

Q.4. Do you think consumers should be able to get a free credit score each year along with their credit report since the score is the most important piece of information used by lenders in making credit decisions?

A.4. CDIA applauds its members and others for their market solutions which make available to consumers unlimited access to credit reports, credit scores, as well as providing additional information which improves a consumer's financial literacy. These market solutions, for example, push alerts to consumer's smart phones when data has changed on their report and also warn consumers when there is a risk of identity theft.

Under the risk-based pricing notice rule, consumers can see the score used by the lender for any type of loan. In addition, many credit card issuers and other providers of personal financial management tools now make scores available for free to consumers.

There is no need to create new score disclosure requirements, as the market has clearly responded with a variety of free options for consumers.

Furthermore, it is important to recognize that most credit scores used in lending decisions are produced by score modeling companies, and not consumer reporting agencies. In addition, many different kinds of lenders use different kinds of scores: a mortgage lender, for example, might prioritize different kinds of information in their custom score than a credit card issuer. Mandating that a credit bureau provide free credit score only addresses a limited portion of the credit scoring marketplace.

Q.5. Do you think the consumer dispute (system) could be improved?

A.5. In a study that CDIA commissioned in 2011, an independent research organization determined that 95 percent of all consumers who participated in the dispute process were satisfied with the outcome. [8] However, we recognize that some consumers have had issues with fixing inaccuracies on their credit reports. We will work with you and others to address any deficiencies in the system.

Q.6. Given the potentially catastrophic impact on a consumer when there is a material error on their credit report and the relatively

---

[7] Report to Congress Under Sections 318 and 319 of the Fair and Accurate Credit Transactions Act of 2003, Dec. 2004, v.

[8] Turner, Michael A., Ph.D., Robin Varghese, Ph.D., Patrick D. Walker, M.A., "U.S. Consumer Credit Reports: Measuring Accuracy and Dispute Impacts", *http://www.perc.net/wp-content/uploads/2013/09/DQreport.pdf*.

small cost to the consumer reporting agencies to provide better customer support, do you think the consumer reporting agencies are doing the most they can do to prevent and correct errors on credit reports?

A.6. Yes. First, CRAs work very hard to prevent errors from appearing on credit reports at all. Aggressive monitoring of the roughly 14,000 data furnishers and prompt investigations of anomalous reporting help us ensure accuracy. And in fact, the national CRAs have been examined annually by the CFPB, and those examinations have not surfaced significant substantive or systemic accuracy problems with any of the three companies, despite the large numbers of complaints in the database. When a consumer reports a problem, we work with the lender as quickly as we can to resolve it. Often these relate to significant disagreements between lender and customer. Other times, if a mistake is discovered, we move as rapidly as possible to correct it.

Q.7. In light of the massive data breach at Equifax and the potential harm of identity theft that millions of Americans now face, do you still believe that we should reduce the penalties for consumer reporting agencies when they harm consumers?

A.7. CDIA has supported legislation to align the Fair Credit Reporting Act with other financial consumer protection laws by capping the amount of statutory damages allowed in class action lawsuits at one percent of a defendant's net worth or $500,000, whichever is less, and eliminating the possibility of punitive damages. This would alleviate the uncertainty of the amount of liability that businesses face in class action lawsuits and provide economic stability for a wide range of impacted businesses by reducing the potential for crippling and catastrophic class action damage awards.

Other financial consumer protection statutes, such as the Electronic Fund Transfer Act (EFTA), the Fair Debt Collection Practices Act (FDCPA), the Equal Credit Opportunity Act (ECOA), and the Truth in Lending Act (TILA) place similar caps on damage amounts in class action litigation. When the FCRA was enacted, it only permitted consumers to seek actual damages and did not permit statutory or punitive damages in a private right of action and, therefore, caps on damage awards were unnecessary. As FCRA class action litigation has become more prevalent, however, Congress should appropriately revisit the liability structure of the FCRA.

Bringing the FCRA in line with other financial consumer protection statutes is especially important in light of the current trend of FCRA class action litigation against employers. In recent years, FCRA class action lawsuits have been filed against businesses from a variety of sectors including fast food restaurants, grocers, retailers, universities, and transportation companies. These employers are particularly victimized by lawsuits where consumer harm is not at issue but rather the allegations are highly technical violations related to their use of consumer reports for employment screening. With the possibility of unlimited damages and grave reputational harm, employers and others often settle instead of defending their practices in court.

Q.8. In CDIA's opinion, who should bear the financial liability for fraud and identity theft that is linked to the Equifax data breach?

A.8. In general, the type of fraud that might occur based on stolen personal identifiers would be "new account fraud," where a criminal would open an account in another person's name in order to illegally benefit from the account. In these cases consumers are held harmless as financial institutions absorb the cost of the fraud and seek redress from there. These cases are adjudicated in a number of settings and we believe that each case should be settled based on the facts of the individual case.

RESPONSES TO WRITTEN QUESTIONS OF CHAIRMAN CRAPO FROM MARC ROTENBERG

Q.1. What is the most effective action a consumer can take to protect against identity theft if the consumer's information has been compromised? Please include a detailed description of the differences between credit freezes, credit locks, and fraud alerts, including how long each takes to activate and deactivate and the relative benefits and drawbacks of each.

A.1. As I stated in my testimony, the central problem is that consumers lack control over their credit reports. The only way to fix this problem is to enact legislation that allows consumers to affirmatively opt-in, i.e., a national credit "freeze," before their credit reports are disclosed to others. The current default settings are backwards. A consumer's credit file is automatically available to anyone unless the consumer takes costly and burdensome steps to prevent access. This increases the risk of identity theft. Credit reporting agencies are not incentivized to make it easy for consumers to freeze or lock their credit because they profit from selling consumer data. Therefore, legislation is necessary protect consumers from identity theft. The market does not solve this problem. With that said, here are the current options that consumers have:

Credit freezes: A credit freeze is the most effective action a consumer can take to protect against identity theft. A credit freeze prevents the release of a consumer's credit report unless the consumer chooses to affirmatively release the report using a PIN number or passphrase, preventing hackers from opening new lines of credit in the consumer's name.[1] However, credit freezes are burdensome and costly.[2] Consumers must contact all three credit bureaus and pay a fee to each company each time they wish to freeze and unfreeze their credit.[3] Equifax has apparently offered free credit freeze services after its breach,[4] but this offer expires January 31, 2018.[5] And consumers must still contact Experian and TransUnion and pay both companies a fee to freeze their credit if

------

[1] Lisa Weintraub Schifferle, "Free Credit Freezes From Equifax", Fed. Trade Comm'n., (Sep. 19, 2017), *https://www.consumer.ftc.gov/blog/2017/09/free-credit-freezes-equifax.*

[2] Rohit Chopra, "What Should I Do About the Massive Data Breach at Equifax?" Consumer Federation of America (Sep. 8, 2017), *http://www.idtheftinfo.org/index.php?option=com content&view=article&id=126&Itemid=10.*

[3] Schifferle, supra, n. 1.

[4] Ron Lieber, "Equifax Calls for Free Credit Locks. Experian's Reply? Nope.", *New York Times*, (Oct. 4, 2017), *https://www.nytimes.com/2017/10/04/your-money/equifax-experian-credit-locks.html*

[5] Lisa Weintraub Schifferle, "Free credit freezes from Equifax", Fed. Trade Comm'n., (Sep. 19, 2017), *https://www.consumer.ftc.gov/blog/2017/09/free-credit-freezes-equifax.*

they wish to protect themselves after the Equifax breach. For most consumers, the cost is $5 to $10 per credit reporting agency each to freeze or unfreeze their credit report, depending on their State's laws. [6] Currently, only four States (Indiana, Maine, North Carolina, and South Carolina) mandate free credit freezes and "thaws," while four other States mandate free credit freezes but allow companies to charge for thaws. [7]

Credit locks: Credit locks are relatively new products. There is still a lot we don't know about credit lock products, and even Andrew Smith admitted in his testimony that he was unfamiliar with them. Based on what we do know, they are similar to credit freezes, but are not as effective. First, a credit lock is only temporary, while a credit freeze is permanent. Equifax began offering "free credit lock products" after the date of the breach, but the Equifax product only locks credit for 12 months. [8] Equifax announced that it will begin offering free lifetime credit locking services in 2018, but we still do not know all the details about this service. [9]

A second reason why a credit freeze is more effective than a lock is that a freeze requires a PIN number to "thaw," or release, one's credit report, whereas many credit locks can be undone by just clicking a button on a website. [10] Also, while some credit lock products are free, TransUnion's product requires consumers to agree to receive targeted advertisements from third parties. [11] Many credit lock products also require consumers to sign forced arbitration clauses. [12]

Third, credit freezes are more effective because they are established by State law. [13] Credit reporting agencies began offering credit freezes in the early 2000s after pressure from State lawmakers and consumer advocates, and freezes are subject to State regulation. [14] Credit locks, on the other hand, have only popped up recently, and these products are not subject to State regulation. [15] Because credit freezes are covered by State law, consumers are protected from any financial liability if their credit account is fraudulently accessed. [16]

Credit bureaus have been pushing consumers into credit lock products after the Equifax breach, citing their convenience: acti-

---

[6] Id.

[7] U.S. PIRG, "Interactive Map Shows Consumers in 42 States Have No Access to Free Credit Freezes" (Oct. 2, 2017), *https://uspirg.org/news/usp/interactive-map-shows-consumers-42-states-have-no-access-free-credit-freezes.*

[8] Id.

[9] Rob Lieber, "3 Weeks Later, Equifax Makes a Peace Offering", *New York Times,* (Sep. 27, 2017) *https://www.nytimes.com/2017/09/27/your-money/equifax-credit-freeze-lock-apology.html?r=O.*

[10] Id.

[11] Id.

[12] Id.

[13] Octavio Blanco, "The Credit Bureaus Are Pushing Consumers To Lock Their Credit Instead of Freeze It, But There Are Reasons To Be Wary", *Consumer Reports,* (Sep. 28, 2017), *https://www.consumerreports.org/credit-bureaus/why-credit-freeze-is-better-than-credit-lock/.*

[14] Lieber, supra, n. 4; "Public Hearing on Security Freeze", New York Senate Standing Committee on Consumer Protection and the Assembly Standing Committee on Consumer Affairs and Protection (Nov. 21, 2015) (written testimony of the Electronic Privacy Information Center), *https://epic.org/privacy/idtheft/nystate11.21.05.html.*

[15] Lieber, supra, n. 4.

[16] Blanco, supra, n. 13.

vating and lifting a credit freeze typically takes 24 to 48 hours.[17] However, credit locks still require a consumer to purchase the service from all three credit bureaus in order to be effective, and Equifax's credit lock also takes 24 to 48 hours to be processed.[18] *Fraud alerts:* A fraud alert is the least protective option, though it should still be freely available to all consumers. Fraud alerts won't freeze the consumer's credit, but they will tell anyone who runs the consumer's credit to notify the consumer before opening a new account.[19] Most fraud alerts are free but they end after 90 days, however there are also "extended" 7-year fraud alerts, which require filing an identity theft report.[20] Fraud alerts are not the most effective tool to prevent identity theft; because they do not prevent a consumer's credit report from being pulled, a criminal may still be able to improperly obtain credit in a consumer's name. On the other hand, a fraud alert well help a consumer identify suspicious activity.

Q.2. Many States have laws requiring credit bureaus to provide credit freezes. Can you describe what these laws generally require and discuss whether it is appropriate for Congress to create a Federal standard?

A.2. State credit freeze laws give consumers the right to place a security freeze on their credit reports. These laws set the fees that credit bureaus are permitted to charge consumers to place and to lift freezes on their credit reports. Generally, there is no charge for identity theft victims and a fee for all others. The fee is typically $10 but is less in some States. Some States also mandate free credit freezes for protected categories of consumers, such as: spouses of identity theft victims, minors, consumers over 65 years of age, active duty military members, and victims of domestic violence.[21] Some States (Maine, South Carolina, Indiana, and North Carolina) have prohibited fees to both place and remove freezes for all of their citizens.[22] State laws also specify the length of the freeze: it can either be permanent (until lifted by the consumer) or it can expire after a certain period of time. In three States, a freeze will automatically expire after 7 years.[23]

Congress should enact Federal baseline legislation that would make free credit freezes the default for all consumers. Fees are more expensive than they appear. In order to be effective, a consumer must place a freeze on her credit report at all three bureaus: Equifax, TransUnion, and Experian. This means that it typically costs consumers $30 to freeze their credit and another $30 to remove the freeze later. A Federal standard prohibiting the credit bureaus from charging consumers for credit "freezes" and "thaws" would give consumers greater control over their personal financial information and prevent companies such as Equifax from profiting from their own malfeasance. Additionally, any Federal standard

---

[17] Id.

[18] Id.

[19] EPIC, "Identity Theft and Domestic Abuse", *https://epic.org/privacy/dv/identitytheft.html.*

[20] Id.

[21] ConsumersUnion, "Consumers Union's Guide to Security Freeze Protection", *http://consumersunion.org/research/consumers-unions-guide-to-security-freeze-protection-2/.*

[22] Id.

[23] Id.

should not preempt State laws. States have long been the innovators for consumer protection and many of the best Federal laws are derived from earlier State experiments. California passed the first data breach notification law in the U.S. in 2002,[24] and now 47 more States, the District of Columbia, Guam, Puerto Rico, and the Virgin Islands have all enacted similar legislation.[25] Federal preemption could have the perverse effect of removing stronger State protections and then expose consumers to higher levels of data breach and identity theft.

RESPONSES TO WRITTEN QUESTIONS OF SENATOR BROWN FROM MARC ROTENBERG

Q.1. In his testimony, Andrew Smith implied that if Americans had the right to make consumer reporting agencies delete their data, consumers would use this right to "selectively delete" negative but accurate information. Do you believe this is a significant risk? To the extent that it is a risk, are there ways in which the law could mitigate the risk?

A.1. The right of individuals to limit access to true private facts is well established in U.S. law. This is done in the financial services sector to give individuals, even those who have suffered bankruptcy, the chance to start over.[1] This is done in the criminal justice system to ensure that potentially stigmatizing information does not create obstacles to employment.[2]

Data brokers do not have a "right" to obtain private facts about American consumers. But consumers should certainly have a right to know what information about them is collected and sold by private businesses. At present, the data broker industry is entirely upside down, recognizing little privacy for consumers, but claiming great secrecy for itself.

Andrew Smith's statements made clear that credit bureaus are concerned about not having every piece of financial information about consumers, yet consumers do not have access to all the data the credit bureaus have collected about them. That is entirely backwards. Even more worrisome is that much of the information that data brokers sell about consumers is itself not accurate. That is where the real risk arises because consumers are denied loans, job, and other opportunities because of errors in credit reports provided by credit reporting agencies.

To mitigate that risk, reform of the credit reporting industry would begin by imposing an accuracy requirement on data brokers.

-----

[24] California S.B. 1386, *http://www.leginfo.ca.gov/pub/01-02/bilUsen/sbl1351-1400/ sbl1386 bill20020926chaptered.pdf.*

[25] National Conference of State Legislatures, "Security Breach Notification Laws" (Apr. 12, 2017), *http://www.ncsl.org/research/telecommunications-and-information-technology/security-breach-notification-laws.aspx.*

[1] The FCRA requires bankruptcies to be removed from credit reports after 10 years. 15 U.S.C. 1681c.

[2] See, e.g., EPIC, "Expungement", *https://epic.org/privacy/expungement/* (Forty-five States and the District of Columbia provide for expungement for some ex-offenders or other similar relief.); G.D. v. Kenny, 15 A. 3d 300,205 NJ 275, *https://epic.org/amicus/gdlvlkenny.html;* See also, National Employment Law Center, "Ban the Box: U.S. Cities, Counties, and States Adopt Fair Hiring Practices", (Aug. 1, 2017), *http://www.nelp.org/publication/ban-the-box-fair-chance-hiring-state-and-local-guide/.*

Q.2. In his testimony, Andrew Smith stated that consumers have access to "all of the information on file about them with consumer reporting agencies." Is that true? Please provide a list of all types of data collected by the three national consumer reporting agencies and their affiliates that is not contained in the free credit report that consumers can obtain under FCRA. How do the consumer reporting agencies collect this data? Is there a risk that these data may be inaccurate or vulnerable to a cybersecurity breach?

A.2. Andrew Smith's statement that consumers have access to "all of the information on file about them with consumer reporting agencies" is false because the credit report that consumers can obtain under FCRA does not contain all of the information about the consumer in possession of the credit reporting agency. The Work Number, an Equifax subsidiary, has a database of 190 million employment and salary records covering more than one-third of U.S. adults. [3] The company collects data from human resources departments that can include weekly paystub information, unemployment claims, and information about insurance and health care providers. [4] This information is not included in the credit reports consumers obtain under the FCRA.

Perhaps the most crucial type of data missing from free credit reports that consumers can obtain under FCRA is credit scores which is used to determine credit ratings. While FCRA gives consumers the right to get their credit score from the national credit reporting companies, companies charge for the scores. [5] Earlier this year the consumer reporting agencies entered a consent agreement with the CFPB for advertising credit scores to consumers as free or costing one dollar and then charging for credit monitoring services. [6] FICO has disclosed the approximate weight of the categories but the relative importance of the categories is not the same for all consumers, particularly for those who have not been using credit long. [7] It currently costs a consumer $59.85 for a report from FICO that contains the credit scores from all three bureaus and a list of the "top factors" that affect their personal FICO scores. [8] FICO charges a $29.95 monthly subscription fee for a product that allows consumers to track changes in their credit scores. [9] There are ways for consumers to access their credit scores for free, such as CreditKarma, but these services are not cost-free; they make their money by collecting still more consumer data and promoting loans and credit cards to consumers based on their financial information. [10] FICO scores are used by 90 percent of top lenders. [11] Con-

---

[3] Bob Sullivan, "Archive: Exclusive: Your Employer May Share Your Salary, and Equifax Might Sell That Data", (March 10, 2016), *https://bobsullivan.net/archive/archive-exclusive-your-employer-may-share-your-salary-and-equifax-might-sell-that-data/*.

[4] Id.

[5] FTC, "Credit Scores", *https://www.consumer.ftc.gov/articles/0152-credit-scores*.

[6] Bob Sullivan, "Equifax, Trans Union Will Pay Fines, Refunds To Settle Charges They Deceptively Marketed Free Credit Scores and Credit Reports", (Jan. 3, 2017), *https://bobsullivan.net/gotchas/equifax-trans-union-will-pay-fines-refunds-to-settle-charges-it-deceptively-marketed-free-credit-scores-and-credit-reports/*.

[7] myFICO, "What's in My FICO Scores", *http://www.myfico.com/credit-education/whats-in-your-credit-score/*.

[8] my FICO, *https://www1.myfico.com/products/onetimereports*.

[9] my FICO, *https://www1.myfico.com/products/fico-credit-monitoring*.

[10] CreditKarma, "About Us", *https://www.creditkarma.com/about*.

[11] myFICO, "What Is a FICO Score?", *http://www.myfico.com/credit-education/credit-report-credit-score-articles/*.

sumers should not have to choose between costly services and invasive profiling to obtain their scores.

Still, it is not possible for us to know the full extent of the data collected by the consumer reporting agencies, because the law only requires them to disclose credit reports, not the complete dossiers they keep on consumers. A more comprehensive data protection approach would allow consumers to know what companies know about them.

Regarding data accuracy, much of the consumer data maintained by the credit reporting agencies is inaccurate. In 2016, the Consumer Financial Protection Bureau received more complaints about credit reports than about any other topic: more than 43,000, or about 23 percent of the total 186,000 complaints. [12] The majority of the complaints about credit reports—about 74 percent—concerned reports of incorrect information. [13] There is a high rate of errors in credit reports that consumers have a right to access under the FCRA. It would stand to reason that errors are more prevalent in data that consumers do not have a legal right to access or correct. An FTC study found that of those consumers with disputed information on their account, 50 percent planned to abandon their dispute. [14] This suggests that the credit bureaus make it too difficult for consumers to correct misinformation on their credit reports, causing many consumers to give up. [15] Greater transparency in the industry is needed to know the extent of these risks.

Regarding the risk of cyberattacks and data breach, the Equifax breach is the latest and most egregious data breach by a credit reporting agency, but the industry has a history of poor cybersecurity practices. This September, Experian failed to protect credit freeze pins. [16] Two years ago Experian exposed the records of 15 million T-Mobile customers, which included names, addresses, SSNs, dates of birth, identification numbers (passport, DL, military ID). [17] Last year identity thieves stole tax and salary data from more than 431,000 people from Equifax. [18] Equifax improperly disclosed credit reports due to "technical error" in a separate incident. [19]

---

[12] Maria Lamagna, "Consumers' No. 1 Complaint: Errors on Their Credit Reports", *MarketWatch* (Jan. 11, 2017), *https://www.marketwatch.com/story/consumers-no-1-complaint-errors-on-their-credit-reports-2017-01-10.*

[13] Id.

[14] FTC, "Report to Congress Under Section 319 of the Fair and Accurate Credit Transactions Act of 2003", (Jan. 2015), *https://www.ftc.gov/system/files/documents/reports/section-319-fair-accurate-credit-transactions-act-2003-sixth-interim-final-report-federal-trade/150121factareport.pdf.*

[15] Bob Sullivan, "Frustrated by Red Tape When Fighting Credit Report Errors, Many Consumers Just Give Up, FTC Study Suggests" (Jan. 26, 2015), *https://bobsullivan.net/gotchas/frustrated-by-red-tape-when-fighting-credit-report-errors-many-consumers-just-give-up-ftc-study-suggests/.*

[16] Brian Krebs, "Experian Site Can Give Anyone Your Credit Freeze PIN", *Krebs on Security* (Sept. 21, 2017), *https://krebsonsecurity.com/2017/09/experian-site-can-give-anyone-your-credit-freeze-pin/.*

[17] Brian Krebs, "Experian Breach Affects 15 Million Consumers", *Krebs on Security* (Oct. 2, 2015), *https://krebsonsecurity.com/2015/10/experian-breach-affects-15-million-consumers/;* U.S. PIRG, "Letter to CFPB and FTC on Experian/T-Mobile Data Breach" (Oct. 8, 2015), *https://uspirg.org/resources/usp/letter-cfpb-ftc-experiant-mobile-data-breach.*

[18] Brian Krebs, "Crooks Grab W-2s From Credit Bureau Equifax", *Krebs on Security* (May 6, 2016), *http://krebsonsecurity.com/2016/05/crooks-grab-w-2s-from-credit-bureau-equifax/.*

[19] "Equifax Discloses Data Breach Due to Technical Error During Software Change" (Apr. 9, 2015), *https://www.databreaches.net/equifax-discloses-data-breach-due-to-technical-error-during-software-change/.*

TransUnion has suffered several breaches through compromised client logins.[20] These are only a few examples of the data breach problem rampant at consumer reporting agencies.[21] Any information held by these agencies is vulnerable to security breaches.

Q.3. In his testimony, Andrew Smith counseled against requiring disclosure related to consumer reporting agencies' use of algorithms, calling it a "question of probabilities and statistics." Is it possible that consumer reporting agencies have used these "probabilities and statistics" to discriminate on the basis of race, sex, sexual orientation, gender identity, or otherwise (e.g., by using certain/actors as a proxy for race)?

A.3. Evidence strongly suggests that consumer scoring mechanisms have widespread discriminatory impacts.[22] Algorithms reflect and reinforce the historical discrimination that is present in the data sets they rely on, as well as the human biases of the individuals who develop them.[23] For example, algorithms used in the criminal justice system to predict recidivism rates are based on data sets that are heavily skewed against black defendants.[24] A 2016 investigation by ProPublica found that one particular scoring system labeled black defendants as future criminals at almost twice the rate of white defendants, and yet these scores were unreliable in actually predicting future crime.[25]

Algorithms have also allowed advertisers to engage in racial targeting. Facebook's algorithms, for example, allowed marketers for the film "Straight Outta Compton" to show different advertisements to users based on their "racial affinity".[26] And there is evidence that Russian interference in the 2016 election involved targeting specific racial groups with racially charged political ads on Facebook.[27]

Algorithms in the consumer lending context may also violate the law.[28] The Equal Credit Opportunity Act prohibits lenders from

---

[20] Privacy Rights Clearinghouse, "TransUnion Data Breaches", *https://www.privacyrights.org/data-breaches?title=transunion.*

[21] See, e.g., Privacy Rights Clearinghouse, "Experian Data Breaches", *https://www.privacyrights.org/data-breaches?title=experian*; DataBreaches.Net, "Equifax Mistakenly Sends Woman 300 Other People's Credit Reports", (Mar. 20, 2015) *https://www.databreaches.net/equifax-mistakenly-sends-woman-300-other-peoples-credit-reports/*; Jose Pagliery, "Your Personal Information Just Isn't Safe", CNN (July 28, 2014), *http://money.cnn.com/2014/07/25/technology/security/target-experian/index.html* (reporting an incident where an individual in Vietnam purchased reports through subsidiary account and sold consumers' information to criminals abroad); Graham Cluley, "Equifax and Transunion Say Hackers Stole Celebrity Credit Reports", Naked Security (Mar. 12, 2013), *https://nakedsecurity.sophos.com/2013/03/12/equifax-and-transunion-say-hackers-stole-celebrity-credit-reports/.*

[22] See, Frank Pasquale, *The Black Box Society* 8 (2015); Danielle Keats Citron and Frank Pasquale, "The Scored Society: Due Process/or Automated Predictions", 89 *Wash. L. Rev.* 1 (2014).

[23] Cathy O'Neil, *Weapons of Math Destruction* (2016).

[24] EPIC, "Algorithms in the Criminal Justice System", *https://epic.org/algorithmic-transparency/crim-justice/.*

[25] Julia Angwin, Jeff Larson, Surya Mattu, and Lauren Kirchner, "Machine Bias", ProPublica, (May 23, 2016), *https://www.propublica.org/article/machine-bias-risk-assessments-in-criminal-sentencing.*

[26] Alex Hem, "Facebook's 'Ethnic Affinity' Advertising Sparks Concerns of Racial Profiling", *The Guardian* (Mar. 22, 2016), *https://www.theguardian.com/technology/2016/mar/22/facebooks-ethnic-affinity-advertising-concerns-racial-profiling.*

[27] Adam Entous, Craig Timberg, and Elizabeth Dwoskin, "Russian Operatives Used Facebook Ads To Exploit America's Racial and Religious Divisions", *Washington Post*, (Sep. 25, 2017), *https://www.washingtonpost.com/business/technology/russian-operatives-used-facebook-ads-to-exploit-divisions-over-black-political-activism-and-muslims/2017/09/25/4a011242-a21b-11e7-adel-76d06ld56efalstory.html?utmlterm=.31a7889a3ca0.*

[28] Citron and Pasquale, supra, n. 47.

basing credit decisions on factors that have a discriminatory impact on protected groups and are unrelated to creditworthiness. [29] In the run-up to the housing crisis, mortgage lenders engaged in widespread targeting of minority borrowers for subprime loans. [30] In subsequent lawsuits, Home Mortgage Disclosure Act data revealed that brokers were basing lending decisions on variables that, although facially race-neutral, had significant discriminatory impacts on equally creditworthy minority borrowers. [31] After the housing bubble burst, this discrimination had catastrophic impacts on minority communities. [32]

If credit reporting agencies are permitted to score consumers using secret, proprietary algorithms, then it is impossible to know whether these algorithms violate the law. Empirical evidence demonstrates that credit scores statistically disadvantage protected groups. [33] Numerous studies have demonstrated that black and Latino communities have lower credit scores as a group than whites. [34] Credit scores by their very nature "bake in and perpetuate past discrimination"; they judge consumers based on their histories and consequently limit or expand their future ability to obtain wealth-building assets such as a home, a small business loan, or even a job. [35] Evidence strongly links the current disparity in assets between white and minority communities to the disparity in credit scores. [36]

Yet current law does not allow regulators or the courts to scrutinize these scores to determine whether they violate ECOA. [37] Although consumers have the right to request their credit scores, they do not have the right to know how this score is determined. ECOA's Regulation B requires lenders to state the "specific reasons" for an adverse lending decision—such as a low credit score— but it does not require the credit reporting agencies to disclose how that credit score was calculated. [38] This means that a credit score might include factors that violate ECOA. And because the credit reporting agencies do not directly interact with consumers, consumers have been unable to maintain lawsuits against the CRAs for violating ECOA. [39] Moreover, using credit scores in the employ-

---

[29] 15 U.S.C. §1601 et seq.

[30] Consumer Fin. Prot. Bureau, "CFPB Director Richard Cordray's Prepared Lecture on Economic Rights as Civil Rights at Michigan State University", (Oct. 10, 2014), *https://www.consumerfinance.gov/about-us/newsroom/cfpb-director-richard-cordrays-prepared-lecture-on-economic-rights-as-civil-rights-at-michigan-state-university/*.

[31] See, e.g., Miller v. Countrywide Bank, N.A., 571 F. Supp. 2d 251 (D. Mass 2008); Ramirez v. GreenPoint Mortg. Funding, Inc., 633 F. Supp. 2d 922 (N.D. Cal. 2008).

[32] CFPB, supra, n. 55.

[33] Citron and Pasquale, supra, n. 47.

[34] See, e.g., Consumer Fin. Prot. Bureau, "Analysis of Differences Between Consumer- and Creditor-Purchased Credit Scores", (Sept. 18, 2012), *http://files.consumerfinance.gov/f/201209\Analysis\Differences\Consumer\Credit.pdf*.

[35] "Past Imperfect: How Credit Scores and Other Analytics 'Bake In' and Perpetuate Past Discrimination", National Consumer Law Center, (May 2016), *https://www.nclc.org/images/pdf/credit\discrimination/Past\Imperfect050616.pdf*.

[36] Id.

[37] Citron and Pasquale, supra, n. 47.

[38] 12 CFR Part 1002; Citron and Pasquale, supra, n. 47.

[39] ECOA only permits borrowers to maintain actions against the entities making the lending decisions. See, e.g., Arikat v. JPMorgan Chase & Co., 430 F. Supp. 2d 1013 (N.D. Cal. 2006). HMDA data merely reports the credit score of the borrower, allowing plaintiffs to determine only whether minority borrowers with equal credit scores received disparate treatment. See, e.g., Miller v. Countrywide, 571 F. Supp. 2d at 254.

ment context may violate Title VII because there is no evidence to suggest that credit history is a valid predictor of job performance.[40]

"Algorithmic transparency" is key to corporate accountability in the data industry.[41] Without legislation requiring companies to disclose their scoring methods, we have no way of knowing whether unlawful discrimination is built into these algorithms that determine opportunities for credit, employment, housing, and more.

Q.4. The Privacy Act of 1974 imposes various restrictions on Federal agencies' collection, maintenance, use, and dissemination of information about individuals. Do these restrictions generally protect individuals' data more than the restrictions imposed on private enterprises? If so, does it make sense that consumers enjoy these protections against the Federal Government but not against private organizations?

A.4. As originally conceived, the Privacy Act of 1974 would have provided privacy protections for databases in the both the public sector and the private sector. However, negotiations with the White House led to the removal of provisions to cover the private sector.[42] As a consequence, individuals in United States generally enjoy stronger privacy protections on data collected by the Federal Government than the private sector, though it is worth noting that the Fair Credit Reporting Act of 1970 preceded the Privacy Act and was viewed at the time as the first modern privacy law, i.e., a response to the growing automation of personal data, in the United States.

The Privacy Act is based on the Code of Fair Information Practices.[43] The FIPs serve as the starting point for modern privacy law. The FIPs assign rights and responsibilities in the collection and use of personal data.[44] Since the data is transferred from the individual to the organization, the responsibilities are necessarily assigned to the organization, such as the business or Government agency, and the rights are given to the individual, as consumer or citizen.

The FIPs appear in many privacy laws in the United States, such as the Privacy Act of 1974. The FIPS are also found in privacy laws and frameworks, such as the Organization for Economic Cooperation and Development (OECD) Privacy Guidelines[45] and the European Commission's Data Protection Regulation.[46] Paradoxically, this common approach to privacy protection helps enable international data transfer.

---

[40] National Consumer Law Center, supra, n. 60.

[41] EPIC, "Algorithmic Transparency", *https://epic.org/algorithmic-transparency/*.

[42] EPIC, "The Privacy Act of 1974, *https://epic.org/privacy/1974act/*; Robert Ellis Smith, "Gerald Ford: Privacy's Godfather", *Forbes* (Jan. 5, 2017), *https://www.forbes.com/2007/01/04/privacy-protection-ford-oped-cxresO105privacy.html*

[43] "The Code of Fair Information Practices", EPIC, *https://epic.org/privacy/consumer/codelfairlinfo.html.*

[44] Marc Rotenberg, "Fair Information Practices and the Architecture of Privacy", 2001 *Stan. Tech. L. Rev.* 1.

[45] "OECD Guidelines on the Protection of Privacy and Trans border Flows of Personal Data", available at *http://www.oecd.org/document/18/0,3343,en—2649l34255l1815186l1l1l1 1,00.html.*

[46] Proposal for a Regulation of the European Parliament and the Council on the protection of individuals with regard to the processing of personal data and the free movement of such data (General Data Protection Regulation), *E.C. COM* (2012) final, (Jan. 25, 2012), available at *http://ex.europa/eu/justice/data-protection/document/review2012/coml2012l11len.pdf.*

The problem today in the U.S. is that technology and business practices have outpaced our legal protection. That is why we are experiencing rocketing levels of data breach, identity theft, and financial fraud. That is also why our trading partners are increasingly apprehensive about sending the personal data of their citizens to the United States.

As the Equifax breach demonstrated, there is an urgent need to update U.S. privacy laws.

Q.5. Would you recommend extending any of the principles embodied in the Privacy Act of 1974, such as the "no disclosure without consent" rule, to private organizations?

A.5. We would recommend extending all of the principles in the Privacy Act to the private sector. The reasons are made clear by the Findings section of the Act. As Congress explained:

1. the privacy of an individual is directly affected by the collection, maintenance, use, and dissemination of personal information by Federal agencies;

2. the increasing use of computers and sophisticated information technology, while essential to the efficient operations of the Government, has greatly magnified the harm to individual privacy that can occur from any collection, maintenance, use, or dissemination of personal information;

3. the opportunities for an individual to secure employment, insurance, and credit, and his right to due process, and other legal protections are endangered by the misuse of certain information systems;

4. the right to privacy is a personal and fundamental right protected by the Constitution of the United States; and

5. in order to protect the privacy of individuals identified in information systems maintained by Federal agencies, it is necessary and proper for the Congress to regulate the collection, maintenance, use, and dissemination of information by such agencies. [47]

The purposes of the Privacy Act, as set out by Congress in 1974, apply equally to private sector record systems:

b. The purpose of this Act * * * is to provide certain safeguards for an individual against an invasion of personal privacy by requiring Federal agencies, except as otherwise provided by law, to—

1. permit an individual to determine what records pertaining to him are collected, maintained, used, or disseminated by such agencies;

2. permit an individual to prevent records pertaining to him obtained by such agencies for a particular purpose from being used or made available for another purpose without his consent;

3. permit an individual to gain access to information pertaining to him in Federal agency records, to have a copy made of all or any portion thereof, and to correct or amend such records;

---

[47] Privacy Act of 1974, 93 P.L. 579; 88 Stat. 1896.

4. collect, maintain, use, or disseminate any record of identifiable personal information in a manner that assures that such action is for a necessary and lawful purpose, that the information is current and accurate for its intended use, and that adequate safeguards are provided to prevent misuse of such information;

5. permit exemptions from the requirements with respect to records provided in this Act * * * and

6. be subject to civil suit for any damages which occur as a result of willful or intentional action which violates any individual's rights under this Act * * *. [48]

There are also innovative approaches to privacy protection that should be adopted. EPIC recently made several recommendations to the Commission on Evidence-based Policymaking, including the adoption of privacy-enhancing techniques (PETs) that minimize or eliminate Personally Identifiable Information, and the use of schemes that leave data with the custodial agencies instead of a central repository. [49] In brief, here are four key practices that should apply to the public and private sectors.

First, when data is collected by Federal agencies, it is generally for a specific purpose and its use is limited to that purpose. When data is collected by private entities, however, it is often sold to third-parties and used by many entities for a multitude of purposes that differ vastly from the original purpose for which it was collected. For example, information originally collected by a student loan servicer will then appear on a person's credit report, and it might then be sold to employment agencies and can eventually serve as the basis to deny that person a job. [50] Regulations should limit the use of data in the private sector to only the purpose for which it was originally collected. Purpose specification and use limitation should apply in both the public and private sector.

Second, private entities should be required to adopt privacy-enhancing techniques such as data minimization to limit the amount of personal data that the entity collects and the length of time that the entity retains that data. Data should also be anonymized or de-identified whenever possible. These techniques help reduce the damage when data breaches occur.

Third, the Privacy Act prohibits the existence of secret Government databases and requires Government agencies to show an individual any records kept on him or her (with broad exceptions for law enforcement activities). [51] However, credit reporting agencies rely on secret algorithms that make it impossible for consumers to know what information is collected about them and how it is used. In accordance with the FIPs, consumers should have access to all the data that is collected about them and should be entitled to know how that data is—used, including the factors that determine a credit scores.

Fourth, one of the most important aspects of the Privacy Act is that it restricts the sharing of information between Government

---

[48] Id.

[49] Commission on Evidence-based Policymaking: Comments of the Electronic Privacy Information Center (Nov. 14, 2016), *https://epic.org/apa/comments/EPIC-CEP-RFC.pdf.*

[50] Cathy O'Neil, *Weapons of Math Destruction* (2016).

[51] EPIC, "The Privacy Act", *https://epic.org/privacy/1974act/.*

agencies. It does this by limiting "matching programs," which it defines as the computerized comparison of databases in order to determine the status, rights, or benefits of the individuals within those systems of records. In the private sector, however, personal data is freely transferred between entities without any regard to individual privacy. In accordance with our recommendation for a national default credit freeze, data brokers should not be permitted to sell or disclose data to third parties without explicit opt-in consent by the consumer.

The Fair Information Practices make equal sense in the private sector as in the public sector. Data breaches have impacted Government and private databases alike, and the more personally identifiable information that exists across numerous databases, the easier it is for hackers to commit identity theft and financial fraud.

Finally, of great concern is the use of an identifier by the private sector that was originally intended only for the recording of pension contributions. As I emphasized in my testimony, the Social Security number was never intended be used as an all-purpose identifier or an authenticator. The widespread use of the Social Security number in the private sector has undoubtedly contributed to the unprecedented levels of identity theft. That is why we recommend prohibiting the use of the Social Security number in the private sector without explicit legal authorization.

———

RESPONSES TO WRITTEN QUESTIONS OF SENATOR BROWN FROM CHRIS JAIKARAN

Q.1. Do consumer reporting agencies or their affiliates collect any information that is not necessarily contained in consumers' FCRA-guaranteed free credit reports? If so, what types of information do they collect? Is there a risk that these data may be inaccurate or vulnerable to a cybersecurity breach?

A.1. CRS was not able to identify in publicly available sources a complete account of the furnishers of information to credit reporting agencies, or the type of information that is furnished. CRS was able to identify elements of a credit report, and potential sources of the information contained in those reports.

According to the Consumer Financial Protection Bureau, information contained in a credit report includes the following information: [1]

- Personally identifiable information such as a person's name, names they have used in the past, current and former addresses, birth date, Social Security number and telephone numbers;
- Credit history information such as current and former credit accounts and types (e.g., mortgages, credit cards, etc.), credit limits, account balances, payment histories, dates accounts were opened and closed, and information on the creditor;
- Collections information such as an account that currently is, or was, in a collections process;

---

[1] The Consumer Financial Protection Bureau, "What Is a Credit Report", webpage, June 8, 2017, at *https://www.consumerfinance.gov/ask-cfpb/what-is-a-credit-report-en-309/*.

- Public records information such as liens, foreclosures, bank-ruptcies, civil suits, or judgments against a consumer; and
- Credit reports may also contain a list of companies that have sought inquires or accessed a credit report.

According to the Federal Reserve, however, the above data is only contained in the report, and the credit reporting company may have additional data on a consumer. The credit reporting agencies receive credit information on consumers from banks, credit unions, retailers, utility companies (e.g., oil, gas, electricity, and water), medical companies and collections agencies. Some of the information reported to credit reporting agencies may include non-credit-related information. The information reported to credit reporting agencies by the furnishers may be incomplete. Credit reporting agencies may also collect non-credit-related information from public records or third parties who aggregate public record information. This information assists in distinguishing a particular consumer from another. For example, non-credit-related information collected by the credit reporting agencies may include driver's license numbers. Equifax reported that driver's license numbers were among the accessed information in their data breach. [2]

The data collected by these entities does come with a risk that the data is inaccurate as the data is submitted to the credit reporting agencies by the furnishers and may be inaccurate upon submission or be made out of date soon after submission. [3]

In addition to providing credit reports to consumers and credit information to financial institutions, credit reporting agencies may use additional, identifying information about consumers to develop authentication services for companies seeking to verify that a consumer is who they purport to be. This form of authentication, also known as identity-proofing or knowledge-based authentication, seeks to verify a consumer through that consumer answering questions only the consumer would have a high likelihood of knowing. Such information may include date of birth, Social Security number, address where the consumer has resided, and driver's license number.

Because the credit reporting agencies hold this data digitally, the data is at risk of a cybersecurity breach. The type and extent of that risk, and the ways the credit reporting agencies may mitigate cybersecurity risks they face is difficult to assess without fully understanding the credit reporting agencies' system architecture and data model. The system architecture will inform the entity of how they have built their systems, what versions of hardware and software run on their networks, and how their information technology connects. The data model will inform the entity of what data they have, how they acquire that data, what data they generate, and where their data flows. Understanding those would help develop a data-centric threat model to assess risks, develop ways to address potential attacks against that data, and defend against them.

---

[2] Equifax, "Equifax Announces Cybersecurity Incident Involving Consumer Information", webpage, September 7, 2017, at *https://www.equifaxsecurity2017.com/2017/09/07/equifax-announces-cybersecurity-incident-involving-consumer-information/*.

[3] The Federal Reserve, "An Overview of Consumer Data and Credit Reporting", The Federal Reserve Bulletin, February 2003, pp 47-73.

Q.2. What kinds of technological solutions to the GDPR's compliance requirements exist? More generally, how can companies leverage technology to comply with privacy regulations and protect consumers' personal information?

A.2. The General Data Protection Regulation (GDPR) was approved by the European Union (EU) Parliament on April 14, 2016, and will go into enforceable effect on May 25, 2018. The GDPR establishes consumer rights to data and regulations for how data shall be treated by companies. The GDPR establishes the following requirements for data on entities using and processing data on EU citizens: [4]

- The regulation applies to data on EU citizens, regardless of whether the entity processing that data is in the EU or not;
- Penalties for breaching the terms of the GDPR can be up to 4 percent of the company's annual profit, or 20 million euros, whichever is greater;
- Consumers must receive clear, plain language consent agreements, and must be able to withdraw their consent in a way that is as easy for them to give it; and
- Entities collecting and processing data on EU citizens must consider privacy of that data by design, rather than adding privacy protection onto built systems.

EU citizens (who the GDPR calls "data subjects") also have additional rights to their data, which include the following: [5]

- Data subjects must be informed if their data is breached in a manner that is likely to result in a risk that their rights and freedoms may be infringed within 72 hours of the entity first becoming aware of the breach;
- Data subjects have the right to access any data that an entity has collected or created on them, free of charge;
- Data subjects have a right to have data about them, that is hosted by an entity, be deleted, otherwise known as the "Right to be Forgotten"; and
- Data subjects have a right to extract their data from one entity and port it over to another in a commonly used format.

Commercially available solutions for complying with GDPR requirements exist today. The following are examples of such solutions that may help an entity comply with GDPR requirements:

- Systems that can identify and manage data;
- Systems to authenticate and manage access to data;
- Encryption technology and key management systems to limit unauthorized access to data;
- Systems to track interactions with data subjects, so they can provide consent, request review and edits of their data, or deletion of their data; and
- Software and hardware that sit on an entity's network to monitor the network and computers for security incidents so as to

---

[4] The European Union, "GDPR Portal", website, *http://www.eugdpr.org/eugdpr.org.html.*
[5] Ibid.

mitigate potential incidents and alert security teams of incidents.

While the commercial market has solutions available to entities so they may adhere to the GDPR, entities must evaluate different technologies and determine which technologies are most suitable for their individual practices. These evaluations and determinations are entity-specific, but may be informed by sector guidance (e.g., health care companies or financial institutions). Additionally, some entities will have greater resources to devote to the application of technology, while others will be constrained. These evaluations may lead to an entity opting not to collect or process certain data to ease the entity's resource burden.

While technology is one aspect of privacy and protecting consumer's personal information, an entity must also determine their processes for data collection and use, understand their business needs for data, and establish policies to govern data within that entity. This exercise also helps an entity understand the risks it faces, and how it may be able to address those risks through processes, in addition to technology.

———

RESPONSES TO WRITTEN QUESTIONS OF SENATOR REED FROM CHRIS JAIKARAN

Q.1. Given the major breaches that have exposed so many Americans' personal information over the past few years, haven't we learned by now that it's better for a company to invest in cybersecurity before a breach, rather than scramble to respond after the fact? Don't companies have more tools than ever—like the NIST Cybersecurity Framework—to act responsibly and improve their cybersecurity now?

A.1. The decision to invest in security measures, whether cyber or physical, is one companies make upon considering various risk factors. Not fully understanding their data model, the threats the data they hold may face, the vulnerabilities in their systems, and the consequences of a cybersecurity incident may lead a company to under- or over-estimate their risks, or the risk mitigation strategies the company currently has in place.

However, going through the exercise of accurately assessing risk allows companies to make cybersecurity decisions in a cost-controlled environment. A company can apply the NIST Framework for Improving Critical Infrastructure Cybersecurity (Cybersecurity Framework) to their business to work through and develop a cybersecurity strategy. [1] The Center for Internet Security, the International Standards Organization, and ISACA also publish cybersecurity frameworks which an entity may use in conjunction with, or in replacement of, the NIST Cybersecurity Framework. [2] Once an entity has developed a cybersecurity strategy, they can then estimate the costs to implement that strategy, and therefore implement that strategy under known costs. However, after a security

———

[1] NIST, "Cybersecurity Framework", webpage, at *https://www.nist.gov/cyberframework*.

[2] Cybersecurity frameworks from these organizations can be found at *https://www.cisecurity.org/controls/*; *https://www.iso.org/standard/54533.html*; and *http://www.isaca.org/cobit/pages/default.aspx*, respectively. ISACA was previously known as the Information Systems Audit and Control Association, but now goes by its acronym only.

incident, the costs of response and recovery may be unforeseen and may not be able to be controlled. From a business operations perspective, developing and implementing a cybersecurity strategy up front provides certainty whereas cybersecurity indictment response and recovery is uncertain.

ADDITIONAL MATERIAL SUPPLIED FOR THE RECORD

LETTER FROM JIM NUSSLE, PRESIDENT AND CHIEF EXECUTIVE OFFICER, CREDIT UNION NATIONAL ASSOCIATION

Credit Union National CUNA Association

Jim Nussle
President & CEO

Phone: 202-508-6745
jnussle@cuna.coop

601 Pennsylvania Avenue NW
South Building, Suite 600
Washington, D.C. 20004-2601

October 17, 2017

The Honorable Mike Crapo
Chairman
Committee on Banking, Housing and
Urban Affairs
United States Senate
Washington, DC 20510

The Honorable Sherrod Brown
Ranking Member
Committee on Banking, Housing and
Urban Affairs
United States Senate
Washington, DC 20510

Dear Chairman Crapo and Ranking Member Brown:

On behalf of America's credit unions, thank you for holding the hearing titled, "Consumer Data Security and the Credit Bureaus." The Credit Union National Association (CUNA) represents America's credit unions and their 110 million members.

As we have noted in a previous letter to this Committee, the massive Equifax data breach has put more than 143 million American consumers at risk by exposing consumers' most personal information along with hundreds of thousands of credit card numbers. Stolen information includes personally identifiable information (PII), including Social Security numbers, birth dates, driver's license numbers and payment card data including credit and debit card numbers.

This breach has harmed and will harm credit unions and their members. Hackers had access to highly sensitive PII and payment card data for months exposing credit unions to damages in replacing members' payment cards, covering fraudulent purchases and taking protective measures to reduce risk of identity theft and loan fraud and assuming financial responsibility for various types of fraudulent activity related to stolen identities and misuse of PII and payment card data.

As egregious as this particular instance was, it's important to remember that it is only the last in a long string of massive data breaches affecting consumers. Big box retailers, other merchants, and insurance companies have all been breached in recent memory. And the risk is not limited to the private sector, either. Many in Congress will recall significant breaches in recent years of personal information at the Office of Personnel Management and the Internal Revenue Service. Bearing these in mind, the massive collection of personal data being conducted as we speak by the Consumer Financial Protection Bureau (CFPB) should also give lawmakers and consumers pause.

As this Committee works to shed light on the impact of the Equifax breach and to ensure consumers are not at further risk, we encourage you and your colleagues to consider the risk to consumers' personal data in other sectors of the economy, including the retail sector, as well as at federal agencies like the CFPB. On behalf of America's credit unions, thank you for holding today's hearing. We look forward to continuing to work with you on this important issue.

Sincerely,

Jim Nussle
President & CEO

LETTER FROM JOHN A. KOSKINEN, COMMISSIONER, INTERNAL REVENUE SERVICE

DEPARTMENT OF THE TREASURY
INTERNAL REVENUE SERVICE
WASHINGTON, D.C. 20224

COMMISSIONER

October 5, 2017

The Honorable Tim Scott
United States Senate
Washington, DC 20510

Dear Senator Scott:

Thank you for your letter dated October 4, 2017, about the recent IRS sole source contract awarded to Equifax. Considering Equifax's recent data breach, you express concern about the contract award and ask that we reconsider our decision.

We had two contracts with Equifax, one to offer credit monitoring services to taxpayers and another involving identity authentication services. The contract for credit monitoring was recompeted and awarded to a new vendor effective October 1. The contract for identity authentication services was recompeted and awarded in July to a new vendor. Due to a protest that is still pending with the U.S. Government Accountability Office, the new contract for identity authentication services is being held in abeyance. The contract with Equifax for these services expired September 30. Thus, on September 29, we entered into an interim, short-term contract with Equifax, which, as the current incumbent, is the only vendor that can provide identity authentication services to the IRS. The only alternative was to shut down all online access to taxpayer accounts, which would affect the many individuals preparing to file returns before their extensions run out on October 16. Shutting down online access would also have impacted victims of Hurricanes Harvey, Irma, and Maria. These taxpayers have an immediate need for tax information and may no longer have paper records on which to rely.

When making the decision to enter into this interim, short-term contract with Equifax, we had already taken important steps to understand and evaluate the impact of the Equifax data breach. Immediately upon notification of the Equifax data breach, we conducted a comprehensive internal review and performed an on-site inspection at the Equifax facility. The on-site inspection confirmed that no IRS data was compromised. Further, analysis of the data that was compromised, with the exception of data relating to 209,000 citizens, was data similar to what had been lost in prior data breaches such as Target and Anthem. In consultation with TIGTA investigators, our overall assessment is that the risk to citizens apart from the 209,000 is no greater than what it was before the breach. Additionally, we have seen no indications of fraud related to Equifax, but we will continue to actively and closely monitor the situation.

We have taken significant steps in recent years to strengthen our tax processing systems to further protect against identity theft and refund fraud. These efforts are part of our Security Summit partnership with state tax administrators and the private-sector tax community.

Our work in this area added new protections for tax returns being filed, including greater authentication measures in our processing systems to verify legitimate tax filers and protect against identity thieves submitting tax returns. These additional fraud filters and cross-checks make it harder for fraudsters with just basic taxpayer information to obtain tax refunds. We specifically designed these safety measures to protect against many of the recent large-scale data breaches, such as Equifax, where criminals obtained basic information such as names and Social Security Numbers.

I hope this information is helpful. I am sending a similar letter to your colleagues. If you have more questions, please contact me, or a member of your staff may call Leonard Oursler, Director, Legislative Affairs, at 202-317-6985.

Sincerely,

John A. Koskinen

LETTER FROM CARRIE R. HUNT, EXECUTIVE VICE PRESIDENT OF GOVERNMENT AFFAIRS AND GENERAL COUNSEL, THE NATIONAL ASSOCIATION OF FEDERALLY-INSURED CREDIT UNIONS

3138 10th Street North
Arlington, VA 22201-2149
703.522.4770 | 800.336.4644
f: 703.524.1082
nafcu@nafcu.org | nafcu.org

National Association of Federally-Insured Credit Unions

October 16, 2017

The Honorable Mike Crapo
Chairman
Committee on Banking, Housing,
 and Urban Affairs
United States Senate
Washington, D.C. 20510

The Honorable Sherrod Brown
Ranking Member
Committee on Banking, Housing,
 and Urban Affairs
United States Senate
Washington, D.C. 20510

Re: Tomorrow's Hearing "Consumer Data Security and the Credit Bureaus"

Dear Chairman Crapo and Ranking Member Brown:

On behalf of the National Association of Federally-Insured Credit Unions (NAFCU), the only trade association exclusively representing the federal interests of our nation's federally-insured credit unions, I write today in conjunction with tomorrow's hearing, "Consumer Data Security and the Credit Bureaus". We appreciate the Committee's continued focus on the Equifax data breach and the need for addressing consumer data security issues at national credit bureaus. As NAFCU has previously communicated to the Committee, there is a need for a national data security standard for entities that collect and store consumers' personal and financial information that are not already subject to the same stringent requirements as depository institutions.

Unfortunately, data breaches have become a constant concern of the American people. Major data breaches now occur with an unacceptable level of regularity. A recent Gallup poll found that 69 percent of U.S. adults are frequently or occasionally concerned about having their credit card information stolen by hackers. These staggering survey results speak for themselves and should demonstrate the need for greater national attention to this issue.

While credit reporting agencies, such as Equifax, are governed by data security standards set forth by the *Gramm-Leach-Bliley Act* (GLBA), they are not examined by a regulator for compliance with these standards in the same manner as depository institutions. Additionally, the recent Equifax breach reportedly occurred through a "known" security vulnerability that software companies had issued a patch to fix several weeks prior. If Equifax had acted to remedy the vulnerability in a reasonable period of time, this breach may not have occurred. When a breached entity knew or should have known about a threat, and fails to act to mitigate it, the negligent company must be held financially liable.

Credit unions suffer steep losses in re-establishing member safety after a data breach like the one at Equifax and are often forced to absorb fraud-related losses in its wake. Credit unions and their members are victims in this breach, as members turn to their credit union for answers and support when such breaches occur. As not-for-profit cooperatives, credit union members are the ones that are ultimately impacted by these costs.

Negligent entities should be held financially liable for any losses that occurred due to breaches on their end so that consumers aren't left holding the bag. When a breach occurs at a credit bureau, depository institutions should be made aware of the breach as soon as practicable so they can proactively monitor affected accounts. Furthermore, compliance by credit bureaus with GLBA and these notification requirements should be examined for, and enforced by, a federal regulator. Finally, any new rules or regulations to implement these recommendations should recognize credit unions' compliance with GLBA and not place any new burdens on them.

On behalf of our nation's credit unions and their more than 110 million members, we thank you for your attention to this important matter. Should you have any questions or require any additional information please contact me or Brad Thaler NAFCU's Vice President of Legislative Affairs, at 703-842-2204 or bthaler@nafcu.org.

Sincerely,

Carrie R. Hunt
Executive Vice President of Government Affairs and General Counsel

cc: Members of the Committee on Banking, Housing, and Urban Affairs